# Eat Smart
## in
# Poland

# *Eat Smart*
## in
# Poland

**How to Decipher the Menu**
**Know the Market Foods**
**&**
**Embark on a Tasting Adventure**

Joan and David Peterson

Illustrated by Susie V. Medaris

**GINKGO PRESS™ INC**

**Madison, Wisconsin**

**Eat Smart in Poland**
Joan B. Peterson and David C. Peterson

Map lettering is by Gail L. Carlson; cover and insert photographs are by Joan Peterson except for insert photograph of creamy kohlrabi soup with chives and photograph of Chef Bernard Luissana, which were kindly provided by Jarosław Madejski, Warsaw, Poland; author photograph is by John Mimikakis.

The quote by James A. Michener from "This Great Big Wonderful World," from the March 1956 issue of Travel-Holiday Magazine, © 1956 by James A. Michener, is reprinted by permission of the William Morris Agency, Inc. on behalf of the author.

**Publisher's Cataloging in Publication**
*(Prepared by Quality Books Inc.)*
Peterson, Joan (Joan B.)
    Eat smart in Poland : how to decipher the menu, know the
market foods and embark on a tasting adventure / by Joan &
David Peterson ; illustrated by Susie V. Medaris. -- 1st ed.
    p. cm.
    Includes bibliographical references and index.
    Preassigned LCCN: 99–76130
    ISBN 0-9641168-5-5

    1. Cookery, Polish. 2. Diet--Poland. 3. Food
habits--Poland. 4. Food--Dictionaries--Polish.
5. Polish language--Dictionaries--Polish.
I. Peterson, David (David C.) II. Title.
TX723.5.P6P48 2000          394.1'09438
                            QBI99-1939

Printed in the United States of America

To Zofia

Her love and knowledge of Polish food
added savor to every page

# Contents

## The Cuisine of Poland     1

An historical survey of the development of Poland's cuisine, a rich fusion of aristocratic and peasant dishes.

## Regional Polish Food     19

A quick tour through Poland to see the variations of cooking styles encountered in traveling throughout the country.

## Tastes of Poland     39

A selection of delicious, easy-to-prepare recipes to try before leaving home.

## Shopping in Poland's Food Markets     63

Tips to increase your savvy in both the exciting outdoor food markets and modern supermarkets.

## Resources    65

A listing of stores carrying hard-to-find Polish foods and of groups that focus on travel to Poland or offer opportunities for person-to-person contact through home visits to gain a deeper understanding of the country, including its cuisine.

## Helpful Phrases    69

Questions in Polish, with English translations, which will assist you in finding, ordering and buying foods or ingredients, particularly regional specialties.

## Menu Guide    73

An extensive listing of menu entries in Polish, with English translations, to make ordering food an easy and immediately rewarding experience.

## Foods and Flavors Guide    105

A comprehensive glossary of ingredients, kitchen utensils and cooking methods in Polish, with English translations.

# Preface

> If you reject the food, ignore the customs, fear the
> religion and avoid the people, you might better
> stay home. You are like a pebble thrown into
> water; you become wet on the surface but you are
> never a part of the water.
> —JAMES A. MICHENER

As inveterate travelers, we have had many adventures around the world.
Except for stints as tour directors for the United Service Organization and
the International 4-H Youth Exchange, we have traveled independently,
relying on our own research and resources. One way we gauge the success of
our trips is how familiar we become with the native cuisine. To us, there is no
more satisfying way to become immersed in a new culture than to mingle with
the local people in the places where they enjoy good food and
conversation, in their favorite neighborhood cafés, restaurants, picnic spots
or outdoor markets. We try to capture the essence of a country through its
food, and seek out unfamiliar ingredients and preparations that provide
scrumptious new tastes. By meandering on foot or navigating on local buses,
we have discovered serendipitously many memorable eating establishments
away from more heavily trafficked tourist areas. As unexpected but
cherished diners, we have had the pleasure of seeing our efforts in learning
the cuisine appreciated by the people in ways that make an understanding of
each other's language unimportant.

Each trip energizes us as though it were our first; the preparation for a visit
becomes almost as exciting as the trip itself. Once we determine the destination,
we begin to accumulate information—buying most, if not all, the current,
relevant guide books, raiding the libraries and sifting through our hefty

collection of travel articles and clippings for useful data. A high priority for us is the creation of a reference list of the foods, with translations, from the gathered resource materials. For all but a handful of popular European destinations, however, the amount of information devoted to food is limited. General travel guides and phrase books contain only an overview of the cuisine because they cover so many other subjects of interest to travelers. Not surprisingly, the reference lists we have compiled from these sources have been inadequate; too many items on menus were unrecognizable. Of course, some menus have translations but these often are more amusing than helpful, and many waiters cannot provide further assistance in interpreting them. Furthermore, small neighborhood establishments—some of our favorite dining spots—frequently lack printed menus and, instead, post their daily offerings, typically in the native language, on chalkboards outside the door. So unless you are adequately familiar with the language of food, you may pass up good tasting experiences!

To make dining a more satisfying cultural experience for ourselves and for others, we resolved on an earlier vacation that we would improve upon the reference lists we always compiled and research the food "on the spot" throughout our next trip. Upon our return, we would generate a comprehensive guidebook, making it easier for future travelers to know the cuisine. The book that resulted from that "next trip" featured the cuisine of Brazil and represented the first in what would be a series of in-depth explorations of the foods of foreign countries; to date we have published four other "Eat Smart" guides. These cover the cuisines of Turkey, Indonesia, Mexico and Poland. Our intention is to enable the traveler to decipher the menu with confidence and shop or browse in the supermarkets and in the fascinating, lively outdoor food and spice markets empowered with greater knowledge.

Our own journeys have been greatly enhanced because we have had new culinary experiences. One of many illustrations of this in Poland occurred in the southeastern region, in Rzeszów, the major city in this area of Poland, and in Baryczka, a small village nearby. Before our departure, Michal Krolewski had phoned ahead to his relatives there and made arrangements for us to enjoy some home cooking with them, knowing that travelers do most of their eating in restaurants.

Michal is director of International Student Services at Saint Mary's College in Orchard Lake, Michigan. This college attracts many Poles, including Michal's assistant, Mariusz Palka, from Rzeszów. Fortunately for us, Mariusz had arrived home in Rzeszów for a vacation a few days before we did and he added some cooking lessons to our activities.

Teresa Palka, Mariusz' mother, was all set to show us how to make *amoniaki* when we joined her early one morning. These are sugar-coated sour cream cookies from the region of Poland called Strzyżów, where Teresa grew up. They are made with an unusual leavening agent, ammonium carbonate. As the cookies bake, they rise to three times their original thickness as ammonia gas is formed and given off. We had the windows open and the oven fan on in case any gas escaped from the oven. These delicious cookies were done when completely dry, and if we hadn't witnessed their preparation, we would not have been able to tell what had caused them to rise. (See color insert, p. 1.) She also demonstrated how to make *prosiaki,* a type of bread labeled as "peasant" food. Small rectangles are cut out of the rolled buttermilk dough and lightly fried in oil. Since we were unlikely to find these foods elsewhere on our travels in Poland, Teresa chose to feature them in our cooking session.

We had lunch the next day in the village of Baryczka where Michal's grandmother, Emilia Bałajewicz, lives. We had just come from the home of Emilia's daughter, Bogusława Bogacka, in Rzeszów, and had eaten several Polish breakfast specialties prepared by Bogusława and her husband, Eugeniusz, followed by a delicious three-layered cheesecake. (See color insert, p. 8 and recipe, p. 56.) When we arrived at Emilia's countryside home, we saw that her homemade noodles were already set out into bowls (see color insert, p. 5) so we hurried to the table. Broth was then added to the noodles and the first course of lunch was on. Between bites we wrote down recipes as Mariusz translated them for us. Emilia and Bogusława rattled off ingredients and cooking instructions from memory. We were especially intrigued by one of the soups Emilia likes to prepare, *polewka z serwatka* (see recipe, p. 47), which is made from the nutritious cheese byproduct, whey. Since Emilia had the necessary soured whole milk at hand, we later went to the kitchen and watched cheese curds form when the milk was boiled. The whey is left when the curds are strained. Watching this process inspired us to try making farmer's cheese when we got home, and to experiment with cooking with whey in our kitchen.

The purpose of our "Eat Smart" guides is to encourage sampling new and often unusual foods. What better way is there to get to know a culture than through its cuisine? Informed travelers, we know, will be more open to experimentation. The guides also will help steer the traveler away from foods they want to avoid—everyone confesses to disliking something!

This guide has four main chapters. The first provides a history of Polish cuisine. It is followed by a chapter with descriptions of regional Polish foods. The other main chapters are extensive listings, placed near the end of the book for easy reference. The *Menu Guide* is an alphabetical compilation of menu entries, including more general Polish fare as well as regional specialties. Some noteworthy, not-to-be-missed dishes with country-wide popularity are labeled "national favorite" in the margin next to the menu entry. Some classic regional dishes of Poland—also not to be missed—are labeled "regional classic." The *Foods & Flavors Guide* contains a translation of food items and terms associated with preparing and serving food. This glossary will be useful in interpreting menus since it is impractical to cover in the *Menu Guide* all the flavors or combinations possible for certain dishes.

Also included in the book is a chapter offering hints on browsing and shopping in the food markets and one with phrases that will be useful in restaurants and food markets to learn more about the foods of Poland. A chapter is devoted to classic Polish recipes. Do take time to experiment with these recipes before departure; it is a wonderful and immediately rewarding way to preview Polish food. Most special Polish ingredients in these recipes can be obtained in the United States; substitutions for unavailable ingredients are given. Sources for hard-to-find Polish ingredients can be found in the *Resources* chapter, which also cites groups that focus on travel to Poland or offer the opportunity to have person-to-person contact through home visits to gain a deeper understanding of the country, including its cuisine.

We call your attention to the order form at the end of the book. The form can be used to order additional copies of this book or any of our other "Eat Smart" guides directly from Ginkgo Press,™ Inc. The back of the form can be used for your comments and suggestions. We would like to hear from you, our readers, about your culinary experiences in Poland. Your comments and suggestions will be helpful for future editions of this book.

*Szczęśliwej podróży i smacznego!*

JOAN AND DAVID PETERSON
Madison, Wisconsin

# Acknowledgments

We gratefully acknowledge those who assisted us in preparing this book. Zofia Kubinski, Robert & Maria Strybel, Wacław Szybalski and Maryann Wojciechowski, for translations; Emilia Bałajewicz, Ewa Bartowiak, Halina Bartowiak, Bogusława Bogacka, Jurek and Aleksandra Burzynski, Marcin Filutowicz, Roma Górnicka, Roman Groszewski, Sophie Hodorowicz Knab, Judy Krauza, Zofia Kubinski, Beata Kuczek, Maciej Kuroń, Bernard Lussiana, Teresa Palka, David Peterson, Zbigniew Sekuła, Wanda Sicińska, Robert and Maria Strybel, and Ela and Andy Wasielewski for contributing recipes from their private collections; Susie V. Medaris for her magical illustrations; Gail Carlson for enlivening our maps with her handwriting; Susan Chwae (Ginkgo Press) for a knockout cover design; Lanita Haag (Widen Enterprises) for the excellent four-color separations; John Mimikakis for a classy photograph of the authors; and Nicol Knappen (Ekeby) for bringing the text neatly to order.

We are indebted to many people for help in identifying regional Polish foods and menu items, suggesting itineraries, and providing source materials or illustration materials. Thanks to Rosemarie Aldin, Jack Badura, Magda Bartkowiak, Suzie and Paul Beckwith, Thomas Bjorkman, Peter Bogucki, Tomasz Cukiernik, Malcolm Davidson, Marcin Filutowicz, Artur Goławski, Roma Górnicka, Tadeusz Jaroszczyk, Sophie Hodorowicz Knab (author, *Polish Customs, Traditions and Folklore*), Andrew Kobos, Richard Kort, Judy Krauza, Michal Krolewski, Zofia Kubinski, Bogusław Majewski, Marcin Maruta, Tim Mello, Marge Micherdzinski, Ted Morawski, Anna and Michal Niewiadomski, Agnieszka Niezbecka, Maria Emma Pikon, Jan Rapacz, Marie Rosa, Dorota Rygiel, Irvin Schick, Larry Schofer, Wanda Sicińska, Kamil Siciński, Rafal Siciński, Dorota Szweda, Wacław Szybalski, Frans Vedder, Agnieszka Wichrowska, Jadwiga Wild and Marcin Żmudzki.

# ACKNOWLEDGMENTS

We'd like to thank the following people for introducing us to regional foods or presenting cooking demonstrations in Poland: Emilia Bałajewicz, Ewa, Jan, Magda and Halina Bartkowiak, Bogusława Bogacka, Eugeniusz Bogacki, Roma Górnicka (editor, *Kuchnia*), Roman Groszewski (owner, Kubicki restaurant, Gdańsk), Dorota Kietlińska, Stanisława and Tadeusz Konopka, Beata Kuczek, Maciej Kuroń, (owner and chef, Studio Buffo restaurant, Warsaw), Bernard Luissana (executive head chef, Le Royal Meridien Bristol, Warsaw), Danuta and Władek Majewski, Robert Maklowicz, Marcin Maruta, Waldemar and Wojciech Muszyński (owners, Retman restaurant, Gdańsk), Mariusz, Teresa and Stanisław Palka, Mary Pinińska (public relations manager, Le Royal Meridien Bristol, Warsaw), Zbigniew Sekuła (executive chef, Wierzynek restaurant, Cracow), Kamil Siciński, Lidia Stankiewicz (owner, Flik restaurant, Warsaw), Robert and Maria Strybel (authors, *Polish Heritage Cookery*), Wojciech Wierba, Marek Vetulani and Katarzyna Wypych.

Thanks also to the members of the Polish Heritage Club in Madison, Wisconsin, members of the Association of Polish-American Professionals Discussion List, members of the Friends of Poland Discussion List, members of the Mniam Discussion List, members of the Poland-L Discussion List, members of the pl.rec.kuchnia Discussion List, Alfred Senn, Jennifer Clearwater (co-ordinator, Milwaukee Polish Fest) and Anne Wal (chairperson, food committee, Milwaukee Polish Fest) for useful information on Poland and Polonia, Leon Lindberg, Norman and Audrey Stahl, whose unofficial newspaper clipping services kept us well-supplied with timely articles about Poland, and Dave Nelson for his unflagging encouragement.

And special thanks to Brook Soltvedt, a most perceptive and helpful editor.

# Eat Smart
## in
# Poland

Poland

# The Cuisine of Poland

## *An Historical Survey*

One has only to look at Poland's geographical position and note the minor topographic features on the eastern and western borders to understand her historic vulnerability to aggressive neighbors. The amazingly resilient Poles had their country annihilated for 123 years after Austria, Prussia and Russia completed their partitioning of it. They outlived the Nazi attempt to leave nothing Polish in Poland. And they emerged from behind the Iron Curtain after four and a half decades of communist control following World War II. Despite wars and occupations, the Polish national consciousness and cultural traditions endure.

Native Polish cookery has absorbed foreign influences in times of peace and strife. When kings wed foreign sovereigns—indeed, when foreigners were elected king—new foods and tastes were introduced at court. And when the country was occupied by foreign armies and controlled by distant governments, the impact was felt in Polish kitchens. As culinary borrowings were adapted to suit Polish tastes, a distinct national cuisine of exceptional quality evolved.

### Early History

Polish land has been farmed since about 4000 BC. Primitive agriculturalists settled first in southern upland areas that had fertile, easily worked soils and later in the lowlands between the Vistula and Odra Rivers in what is known as the North European Plain. The principal crops were barley, millet, rye and several varieties of wheat. Animal husbandry was practiced by this time, and with the domestication of cattle, sheep, goats and pigs, it was possible to have a more dependable supply of meat. Early diets also included fish, waterfowl, wild boar and deer, and wild, edible tubers and berries.

1

Visitors to Poland today can get an idea of what these ancient communities must have been like. A fortified Iron Age island village built by farmers and traders in about 600 BC was discovered by archaeologists in 1933 on the peninsula of Lake Biskupin near Gniezno in western Poland, and much of it has been reconstructed. Named Lusatians because they were first identified in the eastern German region of Lusatia, these settlers built several rows of wooden houses, surrounded their village with a rampart made of wood and sod, and further fortified the community with a breakwater palisade of logs driven into the lake bed at a menacing, oblique angle. Fossil remains found at the site indicate the crops that were grown: broad beans, lentils and peas, wheat, barley, millet, rye, flax, poppies and rapeseed.

About 400 BC the village of Biskupin was sacked by the nomadic, warlike Scythians, who in turn were displaced by the Samartians. Many other cultures migrated to the lands of present-day Poland, in some cases to settle. Slavic peoples who came from the southeast in the 7th and 8th centuries AD are considered the forebears of the Poles.

Among the diverse Slavic groups that settled in various areas of the country was the tribe called Polanie, meaning the "field dwellers." They occupied the lands in the Warta River valley in western Poland near present-day Poznań, an area later known as Wielpolska (Great Poland). This prominent West Slav tribe gave Poland its name. In the 10th century the Polanie conquered Slavic tribes in lands to the south (the territory of the Vislanian tribe, later known as Małopolska, or Little Poland, and Silesia), to the east (Mazovia) and to the north (Kujavia and Pomerania), and united them into the newborn Polish state, which was ruled from the castle town of Gniezno. According to oral tradition, the earliest ruler was Piast, who reigned during the middle of the 9th century and began a dynasty that lasted 500 years.

## The Piast Dynasty (966–1370)

Polish recorded history begins with the acceptance of Christianity in 966 by Duke Mieszko I, leader of the Polanie and a descendent of Piast. This event linked Poland to the political system of Europe and the sphere of Latin literacy. It also averted the threat of German invasions undertaken ostensibly to bring Christianity to the pagans. Within two years the first Polish bishopric was founded in Poznań. Clerics migrated to Poland, especially from France and Italy, and introduced western culture, influenced court policy and administration, and stimulated creative activity.

Ripe seeds of buckwheat, *Fagopyrum esculentum,* a nutritious alternative to potatoes. Dehulled buckwheat seeds (groats), *kasza gryczana,* often are toasted for more robust flavor. They traditionally accompany game and meat entrées and also appear in humble peasant dishes.

Among the earliest chroniclers of the age was Gallus Anonymus, a French Benedictine monk, who in 1116 wrote a history of the Polish state and its ruling house. From him we learn a little more about culinary matters to add to that already gleaned from archaeological finds. He recorded that choice dishes of birds and game were ordinary foods eaten at court. Honey and fish were abundant, as were beer, wine and mead, an alchoholic beverage made by fermenting honey and water. He also described an event that had occurred over 100 years earlier in the year 1000—the opulent reception and three days of feasts provided by Duke Bolesław I, the Brave, son of Duke Mieszko I, in honor of Otto III, the Holy Roman Emperor. The occasion was the latter's visit to Gniezno and his recognition of the autonomy of the Polish See. We learn more about the costly gold and silver platters on the banquet tables, however, than about the foods they contained. One must assume that the cuisine served to Otto III was rich beyond imagination, since everyday meals served to the Duke were themselves declared very sumptuous. According to legend, the menu of these feasts consisted of well-spiced meats, fish and game, fried in honey and served with rich, delicious sauces, along with fruit and spiced cakes. All this was washed down with mead, the drink of the upper classes, and wine.

Certainly Polish chefs preparing dishes for Otto III and his entourage had a large selection of ingredients available to them. Pork, beef and fish were smoked and salted, and huntsmen throughout the realm provided a wide variety of game and birds. There were cheeses, butter and eggs, and many types of *kasza* (groats) made of millet, barley or wheat. The fluffy, cooked grains were seasoned with fruit (especially plums) or dried wild mushrooms. It would be over five hundred years before buckwheat groats, a staple of contemporary Polish cuisine, would be considered more than peasant food. Purée-like soups were made with finely ground millet to which milk, meat stock, egg yolks and spices were added. Vegetables included cabbage and sauerkraut, turnips, cucumbers, onions, carrots, dried peas, broad beans and garlic. In addition to plums there were cherries, apples, pears, apricots and walnuts.

The flavors of these early dishes were enhanced by precious salt and spices. It is likely that ginger, cloves, cinnamon and pepper—treasures from the fabled Spice Islands (Maluku) and other lands in the Far East—were available, at least in wealthy homes, since trade routes were known to cross Polish lands. Ibrahim Ibn Yaqub, a Jewish envoy from Moorish Spain, wrote in the years 965–966 about his travels. According to Yaqub, the city of Moguntiacum (Mainz, Germany) was an entrepôt for spices, supplying much of Europe, and the Polish city of Cracow, which then belonged to the King of Bohemia, was a major hub of Central European trade. Roman merchants in search of amber along the southern Baltic coast also traveled through Poland at least as early as the 1st century AD. They brought Roman and Byzantine culture, including the use of spices as condiments for food.

One of the oldest Polish dishes known, a soup called *kisiel* made with fermented flour, dates back to 997. It was prepared as a Lenten dish for Bolesław I, the Brave, King of Poland. The fermented mixture was strained, and the sour liquid was boiled and mixed with water and honey, or milk and honey if not consumed on a day of fasting. *Żurek,* the widely popular and delicious soup eaten today, has its culinary roots in this ancient concoction. It typically is made with soured ryemeal; a non-Lenten version is cooked with *kiełbasa* (Polish sausage). Over time, the name *kisiel* became associated with a jelly-like dessert, often served with fruit, that was thickened with oat or millet starch. Today potato starch is used to thicken *kisiel.*

Poland experienced intensive colonization by foreigners, mainly German peasants and Jews from western Europe, in the 13th century. Tolerant Poland was a comparative haven for the Jews who were experiencing persecution elsewhere. The Jewish community was granted a royal charter in 1264 by Bolesław V, the Chaste. The charter conferred asylum and certain privileges, and allowed the Jews to develop autonomous communes. German immigrants, escaping overpopulation in their homeland, settled primarily in western Poland at this time. Both Jews and Germans made significant culinary contributions to the Polish menu. The Jews were known for the *kugel*, a baked casserole resembling a pudding, and for fish dishes such as *szczupak faszerowany po żydowsku*, a fancy preparation of jellied, stuffed pike. Among the German contributions were vegetables such as the skirret, a root vegetable no longer common today, strudels (*strucla*) and breaded meat cutlets (*kotlety*). They also introduced several sausages, including blood sausage.

The last of the Piast line, Casimir III, the Great, is assured a celebrated place in Polish culinary history. Through a clever combination of diplomacy

A fanciful old beehive carved out of a tree trunk. Bee keeping has occupied the Poles for centuries. Historically, the drink of fermented honey, *miód pitny* (mead), was restricted primarily to the upper classes and was considered a gift of great importance.

and cuisine, he helped defuse a feud between two European monarchs that otherwise might have led to war and fragmentation of the Holy Roman Empire. This was accomplished during an international congress he convened in 1364 in Cracow (the capital of Poland had moved from Gniezno to Cracow in 1308). The congress was attended by the Holy Roman Emperor, King Charles IV of Bohemia; Louis of Anjou, King of Hungary; King Waldemar IV of Denmark; King Peter of Cyprus; and various lesser nobility. While the agenda concerned general European policy, the participants were primarily concerned with the possibility of mounting a crusade against Egypt, a stance vigorously advocated by King Peter of Cyprus. Also of vital interest was the need to settle an unresolved conflict stemming from a derogatory remark made sometime prior to the congress by Charles IV about Louis' mother, the Hungarian Queen Mother. The difficulties were partially ameliorated by a political marriage joining the two quarreling dynasties. Casimir was instrumental in arranging the union in 1363 of King Charles to King Louis' niece, the Pomeranian princess Elizabeth, who also was Casimir's granddaughter. It wasn't until the congress, however, that the troublesome matter was finally put to rest, in no small part due to the Polish King's lavish hospitality and bountiful kitchen.

The poppy, *Papaver somniferum,* is cultivated extensively in Poland. Seeds are harvested from mature pods and used in baked goods and pastries for their nutty flavor, especially at Christmas time. Poppy seed oil is an edible cooking oil.

The congress lasted for weeks, providing ample time for visiting dignitaries to reciprocate Casimir's pomp and generosity by giving gifts and hosting dinners prepared by their personal chefs who had accompanied them to Cracow. It is reported, however, that nothing could compare with the extravagant repast organized on behalf of Casimir by Mikołaj Wierzynek, treasurer of the royal court and one of the richest men in Cracow. Indeed, no gala event for a long time afterward could escape comparison with this famous banquet held at the Wierzynek home.

How vexing that court records of the elaborate dishes served did not survive the passage of time! The noted French Poet Guillaume de Machaut recorded the entire proceedings of the congress and included but a few, unenlightening verses on its culinary aspect. The poet, no stranger to Cracow, visited the city when he served for several decades as secretary to the father of Charles IV, John of Luxemburg, King of Bohemia. These verses state that one should not ask how magnificently the distinguished guests were plied with victuals, bread and wine—it would be impossible to explain because it was so grand!

The Cracow merchant's home where the memorable feast took place has been incorporated into the setting of one of Poland's finest restaurants, named Wierzynek, of course. A copy of Jan Mateijko's famous painting, "The Feast at Wierzynek's," rendered in the 19th century, can be viewed there.

The Cypriots attending Casimir's congress are noteworthy for having introduced the use of the fork for dining, a custom originating in Byzantium. Personal forks did not come into common use in Poland (and the rest of Europe) until the 1600s. Instead, fingers were the customary tools for eating solid foods; soups and porridges were eaten with spoons. The Cypriots also brought olive oil and sugar to the Polish table. Beginning in the 1300s, Cyprus had become a large producer of sugar cane, and sugar was widely exported.

## The Jagiellonian Dynasty (1382–1572)

In 1386 the size of the Polish nation increased almost fivefold with the marriage of eleven-year-old Jadwiga of Anjou, grandniece of Casimir III, to the much older Jogalia, Grand Duke of the vast, pagan country of Lithuania. Jadwiga's father, King Louis of Hungary, nephew of Casimir, had ruled

Poland through regents after the Polish King died without a legal heir in 1370. As a condition of the alliance with Poland, Jogalia (Jagieło in Polish) and his subjects accepted Christianity. The Polish-Lithuanian union lasted 400 years, further enriching Poland's growing multinational heritage.

Financial registers reveal much about the foods eaten at the Jagiellonian court. In cases where raw materials for a particular meal were itemized, it is possible to construct a possible menu from them and estimate how much food was alloted per person. It is also known that the economy now supported the production of comestibles for the open market, not just for home use.

Food was served according to status—royal court and peasant family alike. The most important people received platters of food first and with their fingers picked over the assortment for the choicest pieces. The dishes were then moved along for others of lower rank. Personal dining plates during this time were trenchers, slices of round, unleavened bread, which would be replaced with fresh ones when they became soaked. Medieval records of a meal for the dowager Queen Katarzyna in 1563 indicate that dinnerware of fine majolica or silver plate had come into use at the time, although trencher bread was used on fasting days.

Jadwiga and her husband had different food preferences and dined apart when not participating in official court functions. Each maintained a separate royal kitchen in Wawel castle in Cracow, with a large staff both on and off the premises, who performed the myriad functions necessary to procure, prepare and serve food for the royal retinues. Jadwiga's more sophisticated palate enjoyed costly imported foods such as rice, sugar, lemons, raisins, figs and almonds. She favored French cuisine and that of the Hungarian court where she was raised, and for a period of time employed a Hungarian chef.

Both Jadwiga and Jagieło ate substantial meals of poultry, meat and game, often spit-roasted, in rich, spicy sauces with nuts and dried fruit. In modern times the manner of cooking with such generously spiced sauces is referred to as Old-Polish style (*staropolsku,* or *po staropolsku*). One can expect to find in such dishes some combination of cloves, ginger, cinnamon, pepper, saffron and caraway along with dried fruits, nuts, honey and poppy seed. For example, Polish gray sauce (*szary sos staropolski*), a sweet-sour mixture that is actually brown, contains pulverized gingerbread, almonds, raisins, wine and caramelized sugar, and is usually served with fresh or smoked tongue, or with carp.

Fish were available fresh, dried, salted and pickled, and appeared on the table with regularity, in part because of numerous days of fasting imposed by the Catholic church at the time. Salmon, herring, cod, carp, trout, walleye and eel, among others, were often poached, fried or served in aspic.

Dishes prepared for the court table utilized an ample selection of fruits and vegetables. Orchards produced sweet and sour cherries, plums, pears, apples and hazelnuts. Wild strawberries, cranberries, rowanberries and raspberries were used to make juices, sometimes fermented. Onions were especially important to the cuisine. Garlic, cucumbers, lettuce, rutabagas, turnips, kale, black radishes, carrots, dried peas, cabbage, beets and leeks were other common vegetables. Dill, marjoram and parsley were used as herbs. Poppy seeds provided oil for cookery on meatless days when lard was banned. They also were a popular filling for cakes. Wild mushrooms were available in season (early spring and late fall) and were greatly relished. Additional menu items included dumplings and noodles made of flour, several types of sausages and cold meats, tripe and *zrazy,* pounded fillets of meat that are either rolled around a filling and stewed or stewed unrolled.

Carp, *Cyprinus carpio,* a welcome addition to the table in Polish households. No Christmas meal would be complete without it. The fish often are kept alive in a tub of cold water for a couple of days before cooking to remove any muddy taste from the lean, meaty flesh.

Several Lithuanian dishes have become part of the Polish culinary repertoire as a result of the Polish-Lithuanian union. *Chłodnik,* or *chłodnik litewski* (Lithuanian *chłodnik*) is a cold summertime soup. It is made with young beets and beet greens, sour milk and beet juice, and various other ingredients such as chopped cucumbers, onions, radishes and parsley. The soup is typically served over sliced or quartered hard-boiled eggs. *Kołduny* is the Lithuanian name for *pierogi*, thin circles of pasta dough topped on one side with sweet or savory fillings, then folded in half, sealed at the edges and boiled. The Lithuanian version consists of small, round or half-round pastas, filled with either mutton and suet, or mushrooms, boiled and served in soup.

Most of what has been recorded about Polish food habits concerns the upper echelons of society—royalty and the wealthiest nobles, the magnates— and those closely associated with this group, though not themselves

Seventeenth-century woodcut of a kitchen in a manor house belonging to a magnate.

aristocrats. The lower classes did without much meat in their diet, and what meat they had was of poor quality. They were more apt to dine on fatty bacon, variety meats, especially tripe, and fish. Some rural poor hunted in manor forests, either bartering crops for their bounty or poaching. The woods also provided wild berries and mushrooms. Turnips, lentils and broad beans were common vegetables. The lower classes ate thick millet porridges or gruels made of coarsely ground seeds, often mixed with milk. These preparations were also made with buckwheat, oats or unripened rye; vegetables and bacon were added occasionally. Farmer's cheese was a nutritious addition to several dishes. The status of many peasant foods ultimately was elevated by incorporation into court cuisine. This fusion of aristocratic and peasant elements is recognizable in the contemporary Polish menu.

During the 1400s, western Europe developed a great demand for grain, and Poland became a major supplier of wheat, rye and oats. Grain was shipped down the Vistula River and loaded onto vessels waiting at the port of Danzig (now Gdańsk) on the Baltic Sea. In 1466 Poland had regained control of the port by defeating the Knights of the Teutonic Order, who had conquered northern Poland two centuries earlier. With free access to the Baltic, Poland became the granary of Europe, providing grain at a fraction of the cost of wheat shipped from the Mediterranean. This large volume of trade continued well into the 17th century.

The Polish menu was infused with many foreign vegetables and greens when Bona Sforza, an Italian princess from Milan, became the second wife of King Zygmunt I, the Old, in 1518. The princess brought the tomato, which had just been introduced to Europe from Mexico by the Spanish conquistadors. The Italians were the first Europeans to accept this New World product. Other edibles brought to Poland included oranges, lemons, pomegranates, olives, figs and chestnuts. In naming some of the produce and herbs now available to them, the Poles used variants of the Italian words: *pomidory* (tomato), *kalafiory* (cauliflower) and *sałata* (salad). Fennel was called Italian dill (*koper włoski*). The close association of vegetables with Italy is especially evident in today's markets, where one typically purchases soup stock vegetables neatly bundled together and labelled *włoszczyzna* (Italian things). Queen Bona Sforza, with the help of the chefs and gardeners accompanying her from Milan, introduced Italian Renaissance cookery—characterized by a reduced emphasis on spices and rich sauces—as well as the art of gilding food, which was intended to mirror the affluence of the aristocracy.

European wild boar, *Sus scrofa,* ancestor to the domestic pig. Its long snout is used for unearthing tubers and roots. Hunting wild boar was once the province of Polish kings and noblemen. Game continues to be popular in Poland today, and is available in many fine restaurants around the country.

## The Era of Elected Kings (1572–1795)

The Jagiellonian dynasty ended in 1572 with the death of the childless King Zygmunt II August. Three years earlier, when it appeared likely that no heir would be produced, a new system of government was devised based on the election of kings. Thus at the king's death the united Polish-Lithuanian Republic came into being. Recall that Poland and Lithuania had been linked since 1382 by a dynastic alliance of the two separate principalities, beginning with the marriage of Princess Jadwiga to Duke Jagiełło of Lithuania. The elective monarchy lasted until 1795, but it was hamstrung by a powerful parliament (Seym) comprised of the nobility, which was wary of central government. About ten percent of the total population was aristocrats, and they had come to enjoy enormous political privileges at the expense of royal authority. Formal agreements delineating royal prerogatives were made between the nobles and the king they elected. The nobles also contrived the right to refuse obedience if the agreements were not kept.

There were eleven elected kings in this period, only four of whom were Poles. Noteworthy in the culinary sense was the reign of the second elected king, Stephen Batory, Duke of Transylvania, who was crowned king in 1576. His wife was Queen Anna Jagiellonka, the last of the Jagiellonian dynasty and sister of Zygmunt II August. She is attributed with elevating one of her favorite foods, buckwheat groats (*kasha gryczana*), from the peasant table to a courtly setting.

Jan III Sobieski, elected king in 1674, added coffee, omelettes and potatoes to the Polish kitchen. He was a brilliant military commander and hero of the 1683 Battle of Vienna. His formidable cavalry of noblemen, the *Husaria,* magnificently attired and bearing the characteristic feathered wings attached to their saddles, defeated the Turks at the gates of Vienna and brought an end to Turkish aggression in Europe. Among the treasures left behind by the retreating Turks were sacks of coffee beans. The new beverage of coffee was not immediately accepted by the Poles. The upper classes took to it first, and in 1724 the first of many cafés opened in Warsaw. The omelette was a culinary addition from Jan Sobieski's French wife. Jan Sobieski obtained potatoes in Vienna and planted them in the Wilanów palace gardens outside Warsaw, which had become the capital of Poland in 1596. His successors, especially August III from Saxony (crowned in 1733), encouraged their widespread use by the peasants when he brought German potato farmers to Poland. The potato replaced millet, which had been the dietary staple of all social classes.

The potato was to play an important economic role in Poland's vodka industry. By the end of the 16th century, spirits were already produced on a large scale. Profitability in the industry was greatly increased when vodka was distilled from potatoes rather than grain. This changeover was already well established during the reign of Stanisław II Augustus (1764–1795), the last king of the royal republic. This king, however, was partial to wine. Most of it was imported, primarily from Hungary, because Poland's climate limited grape growing to a small area.

King Stanisław II Augustus, a devotee of the arts, entertained small groups of writers and artists in the royal quarters on a regular basis, providing his famous royal chef, Paweł Tremo, another venue to showcase his culinary skills. The King savored French cuisine and these meals would also include a French interpretation of classic Polish dishes. He was instrumental in introducing the cultivated mushroom from France.

Since roasted lamb was a favorite of the King, it was a frequent offering at these gatherings, sometimes served with the juniper berry sauce that typically accompanies wild game. The use of this sauce with meat could satisfy a craving for game. The most popular meat of the aristocracy in Poland has always been game, and hunting their privilege. *Bigos* (hunter's stew), the national dish, has been important in Polish cuisine for centuries and its preparation typically followed a hunt. The dish contains a variety of game and other meats, including smoked sausage, cabbage and sauerkraut, and it requires long, slow cooking to thicken. It is served as a main dish or as a hot appetizer, often on toast. *Bigos* is even tastier a day or so after it is prepared.

The first original Polish cookbook was written in 1682 by Stanisław Czerniecki, a nobleman and secretary to King Jan III Sobieski, and is entitled *Compendium Fercolorum Albo Zebranie Potraw* in Latin, or "A Collection of Dishes." The oldest cookbook in existence, however, is entitled *Kuchmistrzostwo* in Polish, or "The Art of Cooking and Cellaring." It is a translation made in 1532 from a German work, and a single copy of it remains today.

Poland's prototype eatery, the *karczma,* had its beginnings in the Middle Ages. A roadside restaurant catering to travelers and local clientele, the *karczma* historically was a place where travelers could change horses and get a bite to eat. Many still flourish in contemporary Poland. (See color insert, p. 2.)

## The Partitions (1795–1918)

Over the course of several centuries, the real power in Poland was exercised by the nobility, specifically the wealthiest, the magnates, who maintained their own armies and fought among themselves to gain additional political advantage. They also courted favor with foreign regimes at the expense of Poland if it suited the interest of their estate. Legislation was in the control of the nobles, and parliament's role as supreme authority in the state was strengthened with the decline in royal jurisdiction. The *liberum veto*—the principle that no legislation could be enacted without complete consensus— was introduced to ensure against both an attempt by the monarchy to exercise absolutism and any loss of the nobility's liberties. In effect, a single dissenting vote dissolved the parliament and paralyzed the central government. The first use of the *liberum veto* occurred in 1652. Forty-eight of the fifty-five parliamentary sessions held between 1652 and 1764 were dissolved—about one third of them by the veto of only one individual. The result was grave internal impotence and decline of the government, which played into the hands of foreign governments with predatory interests in Polish territory.

In 1772 Russia, Prussia and Austria, under self-serving treaty agreements, annexed about 30 percent of Polish territory between them. After the catastrophe of the First Partition, Poland reorganized its entire political structure and enacted comprehensive reforms, including the annullment of the *liberum veto,* in the form of a liberal constitution passed May 3, 1791. Before the reforms could produce significant results, Russia and Prussia, anticipating that the new democracy would be dangerous to them, grabbed more than half of the remaining land in 1793. Two years later, Austria, Russia and Prussia erased Poland from the map by dividing up the remainder. Poland as a political entity evaporated into thin air for 123 years.

After the annihilation of their country, the Poles struggled as best they could to preserve their national identity. They maintained a religious and cultural community despite eradication of their language and suppression of their history. The Catholic church played a pivotal role in keeping the Polish spirit, patriotism and language alive. Revolutionary France was considered the Poles' sole ally, and a government in exile was established there.

Of course, the Poles continued eating during the Partitions. The influence of French cuisine felt in the middle of the 1700s remained appreciable to the end of the 1800s, and French-style preparations, centered on peasant cookery, become integrated with Polish cuisine. This culinary development occurred in the major urban areas of Lwów and Cracow (then part of Austria) and Warsaw (then part of Russia). Influence on the cuisine was also felt from

Old carved cheese press (*prasa do sera*) made of wood. After milk curds are strained from the whey through a cloth sack, they are pressed between two boards to extract more moisture and produce a firm, sliceable farmer's cheese called *twaróg*.

15

the kitchens of the three partitioning powers. The Russian contribution essentially came from the peasant element and was felt primarily in rural areas in Poland's former eastern borderlands. Tea became popular in the Russian sector, often savored with cream or fruit juices—even wine. Germanic contributions in the Prussian- and Austrian-held regions of Poland were also considerable. For the sweet tooth, scrumptious Viennese-style cheesecakes were a welcome addition to the already rich menu of classic Polish cakes and other desserts. The most popular of all Polish cakes, *paczki,* originated in Vienna. This small, round, iced or powdered yeast cake, or doughnut, filled with preserves, quickly became a highly praised dessert to enjoy with coffee in the cafés.

## Recent Times (1918–Present)

World War I brought freedom to Poland at great expense. Some two million Poles fought in the battles, having been drafted in the armies of the three partitioning powers now at war with each other. Tragically, the Poles were obliged to fight each other on Polish soil.

With the founding of The Second Republic on November 11, 1918, independence was restored to the Polish nation. It now faced the daunting task of overturning the legacy of foreign administration in each partition and returning to a normal existence.

Poland's population was predominantly agrarian. Almost half of the land was held in large, private estates by descendents of Polish nobles or owned by the state. It was on these estates that the cuisine of the nobles continued to flourish until World War II, when Nazi Germany and the Soviet Union swallowed the country, placing Poland under occupation once again. Poland's military machine offered fierce resistance, but her allies were unprepared to help, and she was forced to succumb to the invaders. Over 6 million Poles, including almost all the Polish Jews, died in combat or were murdered.

Poland's post-war fate was determined at the Yalta Conference in 1945; the country was handed over to the Soviet Union. Major societal restructuring occurred with the subsequent spread of communism. The imposed agrarian reform eliminated large, landed estates and reduced the number of people employed in agriculture, giving rise to increased urbanization of the Polish people and a change in food habits.

During the communist era, the government subsidized *mleczarnia* (milk bars), cafeterias that served inexpensive vegetarian and milk-based dishes. These have almost faded from existence.

Led by Lech Wałęsa, the shipyard electrician and chairman of the Solidarnść (Solidarity) labor union, Poland's first democratic government after decades of communism was formed in 1989. In 1990, Wałęsa was elected president of the Third Republic of Poland in the first free elections. Wałęsa's new government began the process of steering the country through the difficult transition from a one-party state with a centrally planned economy to a democracy with a market-driven economy.

Visitors to Poland today may be surprised to find an abundance and variety of fresh produce and other foodstuffs in the markets and consumer goods in the shops. This renaissance of a country that only recently shed the drab cloak of communism and the other horrors of its national history is long overdue. Poland today is a stable and vibrant country, and a full member of NATO. Her tourism apparatus is in full gear, and those who enjoy getting to the heart of a culture through its cuisine should know that gastronomic adventures of the first order await travelers choosing Poland as their destination.

Regions of Poland

# Regional Polish Food

## A Quick Tour of Polish Foods and Their Regional Variations

### Polish Food in a Nutshell

Poland's robust, nutritious cuisine reflects rich harvests made possible by fertile soil and moderate climate. In late spring, much of the countryside is covered with fields of grain—wheat, rye, buckwheat, barley and millet—and extensive yellow tracts of blossoming rapeseed plants, whose seeds are an excellent source of cooking oil high in cholesterol-balancing unsaturated fat. By summertime, wild red poppies provide a breathtaking blaze of color dotting the wheat fields. Larger, pinkish-white poppies are cultured for their seeds, an important Polish culinary ingredient.

Agriculture in Poland was not fully collectivized by the communists. Over three-fourths of the arable land was placed in the private sector and the majority of private holdings were relatively small, averaging about 18 acres. It was hardly possible to eke out a living on these small plots. Farms in the southern and eastern regions had less acreage than those in the rest of the country, where collective farms were more numerous.

Post-communist agricultural reforms include setting up large, efficient farms by consolidating smaller ones, increasing the use of modern production methods and privatizing state farms. Additional income for rural inhabitants now comes from agritourism, which is transforming the countryside as farmers develop local tourist facilities on their properties for urbanites and travelers who want to get close to nature on their holidays.

Principal crops on Polish farms, in addition to wheat and other grains, are rapeseed, potatoes and other vegetables, sugar beets, apples, currants and strawberries. The production of livestock includes cattle, sheep, pigs, and chicken.

Foods stemming from the peasant tradition are the most well known Polish edibles outside of the country. The little stuffed pasta pillows (*pierogi*), sausage (*kiełbasa*), hot stuffed cabbage rolls (*gołąbki*) and beet soup (*barszcz*) are immediately recognized as Polish. Courtly dishes on the home or restaurant menu usually remain a marvelous discovery for the visitor to Poland. Hussar-style roast beef (*pieczeń huzarska*) is an excellent example. The roast is sliced when tender, and each slice is partially cut to form a pocket that is then filled with an onion and buttered breadcrumb mixture. The roast is reassembled into its original shape and cooked to heat the stuffing. The dish is named for the Hussars, Polish cavalrymen in the sixteenth to eighteen century, known for their striking uniforms and "winged" saddles in addition to their prowess in battle. *Zrazy à la Radziwiłł,* named for one of the most powerful magnate families, is a dish of pounded beef cutlets wrapped around a stuffing of bacon, mushrooms, sautéed onions, and pickle strips, and served with sauce inside a small, hollowed-out loaf of dark bread.

Tart flavors are particularly popular with Poles. A variety of foods are allowed to sour naturally to develop the desired tangy taste. They include milk products, rye flour (ryemeal) and beets. Even pickle juice is prized and

*Pierogi,* thin circles of pasta dough topped on one side with sweet or savory fillings, then folded in half, sealed at the edges and boiled. Typical fillings are meat, sauerkraut, potatoes, cheese and fruit. Savory ones often are topped with crispy bits of bacon or salt pork.

forms the basis of pickle soup. The juice ought to be from brine-cured not vinegar-cured pickles. Pickled vegetables, especially cabbage, are key food items. Souring agents such as citric acid crystals are also used to provide tartness when the cook is hurried. The influence of soured foods derives in part from the need to extend the storage life of foods prior to the advent of refrigeration. Souring also has health benefits. Milk sugars in sour milk, sour cream and buttermilk are broken down to lactic acid by friendly bacteria, which is beneficial to the digestive tract.

Polish cookery is not hot and spicy. Fresh dill is the most commonly used herb, and a dill plant is never too far from the kitchen. Parsley, marjoram and caraway are also widely used. For game, dried juniper berries are a key ingredient in the sauce or marinade.

Breads have always been important in the national cuisine. Whole-grain loaves made with coarsely milled grains, once the province of the peasant, are part of a large family of rich, crusty loaves, from dark pumpernickel to white. Sourdough rye is a special favorite. Breads rarely baked anymore can be sampled at some of the open-air museums (*skansen*) scattered around the country that re-create former rural life. (See color insert, p. 4.)

Various cereal grains such as buckwheat, barley and millet appear on the table in many forms. Hulled buckwheat grains (groats) are the most highly regarded and often are toasted to makes them more flavorful. The groats, boiled and baked, typically accompany meat dishes such as roasts and beef rolls (*zrazy*), and wild game. They also become stuffings, pie fillings, and an ingredient in blood sausage. Old peasant cereal mushes that had fallen out of favor are returning to the menus of those concerned about increasing their intake of fiber.

Appetizers include a wide array of delectable and eye-pleasing morsels, typically served with well-chilled Polish vodka. Cold appetizers precede hot ones and each category has both stand-up finger food and heartier dishes eaten while seated. Appetizers in aspic (*w galarecie*) are very popular. Many restaurants have glass-sided display cabinets showcasing whole fish surrounded by a layer of aspic that is artfully embellished with colorful garnishes. One can also order several types of pâté (*pasztet*), herring (*śledź*) served with various sauces and chopped onions, smoked fish and meat, and still have sampled only a few of the myriad cold appetizers found on Polish tables. The most noteworthy hot appetizer is hunter's stew (*bigos*). This thick blend of cabbage and sauerkraut, and a variety of meats, game and sausage is Poland's national dish. (See recipe, p. 40.) Also representative of this subset of appetizers is stuffed eggs (*jaja faszerowane*) prepared in the shell the classic Polish way. (See recipe, p. 41.)

Poles are passionate about soup. The main meal of the day (*obiad*) routinely starts with a bowl of soup. Beetroot soup (*barszcz*) is a traditional favorite. Before beets were cultivated, *barszcz* apparently was made from roots of the wild plant, which were sour. To duplicate the sour taste, which cultivated beets lack, the beet juice was fermented. Today many cooks sidestep this fermentation process by using instant souring agents such vinegar, lemon juice, citric acid crystals or bottled beet sour. Both clear and creamy varieties of the soup are made. Christmas Eve menus traditionally feature clear beetroot soup served with small, mushroom-filled pastas (*uszka*). A delicious early summer soup (*botwina*) is made with baby beetroots and greens. *Chłodnik* is a cold, summertime soup made with beets and other raw vegetables. Other popular Polish soups are *żurek,* which is made with fermented ryemeal and served over quartered, hard-boiled eggs; *krupnik,* a vegetable barley soup; and *grochówka,* pea soup. All sorts of noodles, dumplings and other garnishes are added to soups, and small pastries are served on the side.

Pork is the favorite meat in Poland. The most common pork dish is the cutlet, and most Poles would choose it breaded (*kotlet schabowy*). Also popular are pig's knuckles (*golonka*) and pork loin stuffed with prunes (*schab z śliwkami*). Steak tartare (*befsztyk tatarski*) and beef roll-ups (*zrazy; see* recipe, p. 53) are among the most popular preparations of beef. Traditional poultry dishes include marjoram-flavored roasted duck stuffed with apples (*kaczka pieczona z jabłkami*). (See recipe, p. 52). While game ranks quite high among Poles, most find it more accessible in restaurants than by their own hand. Excellent preparations of partridge, pheasant, hare and wild boar can be savored. Hare pâté (*pasztet z zająca*) is typical fare during the Christmas holiday season.

Polish sausage (*kiełbasa*), commonly encountered in the United States, is best bought in the butcher shops of ethnic markets in Polish neighborhoods, which adhere to the traditional recipes. *Kiełbasa* is actually the generic word for sausage, and many varieties exist. (See recipe, p. 60.) Favorites include hunter's sausage (*myśliwska*), a beef and pork sausage flavored with ground juniper berries and cured in juniper smoke. It typically is eaten cold. Also popular is *kabanosy,* a long, thin, dry-smoked pork sausage, also eaten cold.

Carp and herring are much-appreciated fish in Poland. Both are traditional additions to the Christmas Eve repast (*wigilia*). Carp are fried, stuffed, encased in aspic, or served in Polish gray sauce, a sweet-sour sauce with almonds and raisins.

Staple vegetables include cabbage, potatoes, carrots, beets, beans, dried peas, tomatoes, cucumbers, cauliflower, turnips and onions prepared in simple ways. They often are steamed or simmered, and garnished with chopped fresh dill or topped with toasted, buttered breadcrumbs (the classic Polonaise topping; see recipe for cauliflower Polonaise, p. 54). Hardly a meal is prepared without a dish of potatoes. Even dumplings and pancakes, which Poles serve in many creative varieties, are often made with this perennial favorite. A recipe for *kopytki,* dumplings cut from sausage-like rolls of potato-containing dough, is on p. 54.

The Poles avidly hunt wild mushrooms and delight in their pungent taste, which is more intense when dried. The most prized mushroom is the king bolete (*borowik*), but others of great importance are the golden chanterelle (*kurka*), the milky cap (*rydz*) and the morel (*smardz*). Mushrooms are flavorful additions to stuffings, sauces, gravies and soups, but also can be enjoyed pickled and brine-cured. The cultivated mushroom (*pieczarka*), the common button mushroom in the United States, is also used in Polish cookery.

Wild mushrooms, a signature ingredient of Polish cuisine. From left to right: *smardz* (morel), *Morchella esculenta; rydz* (milky cap), *Lactarius deliciosus; borowik* (king bolete), *Boletus edulis;* and *kurka* (golden chanterelle), *Cantharellus cibarius.*

Polish markets display ripe, luscious fruit. Among the favorites eagerly awaited in the spring is the tiny, wild or alpine strawberry (*poziomka*), whose availability is unpredictable. Interestingly, the plum grown in Poland is called a "Hungarian plum" (*śliwka węgierka*) for reasons no one recalls. Many of the fruits are served fresh with a sprinkle of sugar or in compotes, simple desserts of fruit in a light sugar syrup. Black currant juice (*sok z czarnej porzeczki*) is especially prized. The cake category includes the popular *szarlotka,* which is made with apples. Poles also like to combine meat with fruit. Roasted pork with prunes (*schab pieczony ze śliwkami*) and duck stuffed with apples (*kaczka pieczona z jabłkami*) are luscious examples.

Salads accompany the hot dinner entrée and are made with fresh salad greens, in season, and raw or pickled vegetables. The most common salad, *bukiet surówek,* is a medley of a few shredded, raw or pickled vegetables, such as cabbage, carrots, pickles and radishes, and is available all year. Another popular salad is *mizeria*—thinly sliced cucumbers in a dressing of sour cream. (See recipe, p. 50.) Common dressings are vegetable oil and freshly squeezed lemon juice, vinegar and sour cream. Garnishes typically are fresh dill and parsley.

Dairy products are crucial to Polish cookery. Among these are the much relished fermented milk products such as sour cream, sour milk and buttermilk. Fresh white curd, or farmer's cheese, is readily made from sour milk. The curds are strained through a sieve and eaten without further ado or are pressed between boards to extract more moisture. This cheese is amazingly easy to make. When pressed cheese is ground in a food processor, it becomes a rich, smooth paste that is the basis for cheesecakes and cheese fillings. Curds also are added to many dishes and serve as toppings in even more. A recipe for cheese soup (*polewka z serwatki*) made with whey and fresh cheese curds produced from sour milk is on p. 47. Sour cream is also a staple in the kitchen. It provides creaminess to soups and hot dishes, and is used in baking and as a topping for many different categories of food.

Poland offers a wide range of tempting desserts. Holiday and special-occasion cakes called *babka* are justly famous. These sweet yeast cakes are made in a traditional fluted tube pan that is wider than it is high and narrower on top. A flat, rectangular or square cake (*mazurek*), usually no more than an inch high, is typically associated with Easter but is savored year round. The flaky bottom crust can have a great assortment of toppings, such as jam, ground nuts or poppy seeds, one of Poland's favorite dessert fillings. Instead of a flaky dough crust, the bottom layer can be a ready-made wafer sheet. A recipe for *mazurek* with a wafer bottom topped with a ground walnut mixture covered with meringue (*mazurek orzechowy*) is on p. 59. Cheesecakes made with Polish farmer's cheese are heavenly and two recipes are included in this book; see pp. 55, 56. Puff pastry dough is used to make both individual cream puffs and cream-filled, layered desserts (*kremówki*) cut into squares. The latter is a favorite of the Polish Pope, John Paul II. Filled, raised doughnuts (*pączki*), fried and glazed with icing or dusted with powdered sugar, are traditional favorites and pre-Lenten treats. Fillings include plum, prune and rosehip preserves. Another well-loved pre-Lenten fried pastry is the fancy tri-layered carnival rosette (*róże karnawałowe*).

Tea surpasses coffee as the most desirable hot beverage. Tea is typically prepared as a strong infusion (*esencja*) that is diluted to the drinker's taste or hot water is added to loose tea leaves in a glass. Coffee is steamed and filtered (*kawa espresso*) or prepared by adding hot water to a cup or glass with coarse grounds in it (*kawa turecka*). Tea leaves or coffee grounds that float on the surface or accumulate on the edges of a cup or glass, however, are rather annoying. Drinks made from fruits stewed in sugar water (*kompoty*) are also popular. Several good regional Polish beers are readily available in restaurants, cafes and liquor stores, but most of the wine is imported, since the climate is

*Baba,* a holiday and special-occasion sweet yeast cake made in a traditional, fluted tube pan that is wider than it is high and narrower on top. A smaller, similarly shaped cake is called *babka.*

not particularly suitable for growing grapes. Honey wine (*miód pitny*), made by fermenting a mixture of honey and water, and honey liqueur (*krupnik*) are delicious Polish alcoholic products as are the top-quality flavored and unflavored vodkas that are distilled there. They are drunk neat and well-chilled, preferably in small glasses. An unusual flavored offering is *żubrówka,* vodka bottled with a blade of the aromatic grass on which bison feed.

## The Regions of Poland

A study of Poland's regional food differences must take into consideration the frequent border changes and cultural alignments that have occurred in the past. Few countries have had their frontiers shift as extensively. Poland sprawled over 450,000 square miles at the end of the 15th century, did not exist at the close of the 18th century, was resurrected after World War I with about 150,000 square miles and occupied about 120,000 square miles after World War II. At times she was landlocked, having lost her access to the Baltic Sea.

In the 20th century alone, two major territorial upheavals affected Poland. An independent Poland was rebuilt after World War I from the lands Russia, Prussia and Austria had carved out of her at the close of the 18th century. After World War II the Polish nation was shifted about 200 miles to the west, her fate a consequence of earlier deliberations at Yalta by the Big Three— Churchill, Roosevelt and Stalin. This shift of national boundaries caused massive reshuffling of populations—involving both Poles and non-Poles— who effectively became instant residents of another country. It also allowed Poland to recover some ancient, formerly Polish provinces in the process. Large groups of Poles outside Polish frontiers found themselves once again within Poland.

With a few exceptions noted in the section below, Poland's geography has not played a central role in determining food habits. The country is small, about the size of New Mexico. Except for her mountainous southern aspect, the lowland soils on which the majority of agriculture takes place are not sufficiently varied to greatly limit the growth of many crops to specific regions. One of the more obvious differences between regions is size of arable plot. In the east, plots are much smaller; strips are sometimes only a few feet wide. Regional food differences often are simply local variations of a national dish.

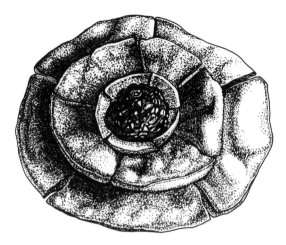

The carnival rosette (*róże karnawałowe*), a fancy, trilayered fried pastry. It is a traditional pre-Lenten treat topped with jam or a cherry.

## Wielkopolska (Great Poland)

The region of Wielkopolska is situated in west central Poland on flat, fertile lowlands drained by the Warta River, the main tributary of the Odra River. This region, together with Małopolska (Little Poland), was the historical center of the Polish state in the late 10th century. Wielkopolska has always been an important agricultural area. It also is a great industrial and trade center. The area's major city, Poznań, is situated on the Warta River.

As a result of the Second Partition of Poland in 1793, Wielkopolska became Prussian territory, and intensive German colonization occurred, primarily in the northern and western districts. The region and the town of Poznań were renamed Posen. At the end of World War I, most of the territory of Posen became part of independent Poland. After World War II, Poland regained additional territory of the former Posen. Large numbers of German residents, now finding themselves no longer on German soil, emigrated to Germany, and Polish refugees from all regions of the country, who had worked in Germany as enslaved or forced laborers under the Third Reich, moved in to replace them. There was also a large influx of Poles who had been forcibly relocated from eastern lands taken by the Soviet Union.

One of the regional specialties of Wielkopolska is a soft, uncooked sausage from Poznań called *metka* or *kiełbasa tatarowa*. It is spread on bread. Some typical dishes of the area are *fasolka szparagowa po poznańsku,* Poznań-style wax beans simmered in milk thickened with flour, and *kwas,* a sweet-sour pork and prune soup also called *kwaśne. Marcinki* are crescent rolls filled with a mixture of white poppy seeds. They traditionally are eaten at the beginning of Advent on St. Martin's day in the western part of the region.

## Małopolska (*Little Poland*)

Małopolska lies in southeastern Poland. This region includes fertile lowlands, the valleys of the San and upper Vistula Rivers, several upland areas, and the Carpathian Mountains and their foothills. Cracow, the nation's capital from 1038 to 1596 and the most important cultural center, is located here. Another major city is Lublin, the largest metropolis east of the Vistula River. Picturesque Zakopane, Poland's highest city, is a prime tourist destination in a scenic valley in the foothills of the Tatra Mountains, the largest peaks in the Carpathian Mountain chain. Charming multi-gabled, four- or five-storied homes are scattered up and down the hills. The section of the Carpathian foothills from Zakopane to Nowy Targ is called Podhale.

The Austrian Empire annexed Małopolska during the First (1772) and Third (1795) Partitions of Poland. This area and Ruthenia, also acquired during the Partitions, became known as Galicia. Ruthenia comprised the eastern half of Galicia and its inhabitants were mainly Ukrainians. In addition to

Large, hand-carved wooden kitchen spoons. Poland has a rich tradition of folk arts and crafts. Items can be purchased at open-air, ethnographic museums (*skansen*) scattered around the country and Cepelia shops in many of the larger cities.

large populations of Poles and Ukrainians, there were minority populations of Jews and Germans. Galicia was situated just north of the Carpathian Mountains, extending from Cracow in the west to Romania in the southeast. It was an impoverished area and many Polish peasants emigrated to America to survive. Galicia came under Polish domination following World War I. The eastern section of the former territory of Galicia, however, was annexed by the Soviet Union (Ukraine) after World War II. Poles residing in this part of Galicia were deported to Poland, primarily to eastern German lands under Polish administration after World War II. Great numbers of evicted Poles living in Galicia's essentially Polish capital of Łwów settled in Wrocław in Silesia. Ukrainians residing in parts of the former territory of Galicia that remained in Polish hands either were expelled to Ukraine or moved elsewhere in Poland.

The Gorce and Tatra Mountains in Podhale are home to a unique culture of highlanders (*górale*). Zakopane is the principal town in the region. The highlanders, who still maintain their folkways, traditionally are shepherds. They raise a special breed of mountain sheep. Ewe's milk is made into a cheese called *oszczypek* (*oscypek* in the highlanders' dialect), which is sold in the village markets. Carved wooden molds are used to give it a spindle shape with a decorative band at the middle and at each conical end. The cheese is then soaked in brine and slowly smoked on shelves under the roofs of mountain cottages to produce a brown-skinned cheese with rich, smoked flavor. A softer, spreadable and somewhat granular cheese, *bryndza,* is also made. The regional diet relies on potatoes, rye and the local cheese, which is not readily available elsewhere in Poland.

The area's menu has many entries based on the local cheese. *Bryndzowe hałuski* are dumplings made from *bryndza* and grated raw potatoes. *Pstrąg po podhalańsku* is a dish of Podhale-style fried trout coated with melted sheep's cheese. *Półmisek serów bacowski* is a shepherd's plate of sheep's milk cheese with bread and butter. Other regional specialties to try are *hałuski z skwarkami,* unfilled potato pasta topped with cracklings; *kwaśnica z ziemniakami,* sauerkraut soup with lamb and potatoes, flavored with caraway; *moskol juhaski,* a bread-like potato pancake topped with butter and *kefir,* a yogurt-like milk product; and *moskol pański,* a bread-like potato pancake topped with ham, mushrooms and grated cheese. A specialty of the small village of Łomnica is *pierogi łomnickie,* rye flour and potato *pierogi* filled with *bryndza*—salty, white sheep's cheese—then boiled and served with butter.

Cracow is associated with buckwheat groats made from finely milled buckwheat and *maczanka po krakowsku,* beef with caraway in bread. Also special to Cracow is *żurek krakowski,* Cracow-style ryemeal soup, lightly flavored with marjoram and served over sliced hard-boiled eggs. From carts scattered around the city, vendors sell Cracow's favorite street food, *obwarzanki,* or ring-shaped rolls sprinkled with poppy seeds. (See color insert, p. 2.) *Kwaśna zyntyca,* a drink made of sour whey, is popular both in Cracow and the Tatra Mountain area.

The Lublin area is an important agricultural area with rich soil. There are many fruit orchards and berry-growing plots. Hops are also a big crop here. Awesome cage-like structures designed to maximize vine growth are scattered around the surrounding countryside. Each cage consists of wooden poles 15 or more feet high, positioned in several rows with several poles to a row. Stout wire runs diagonally from the base to the tops of the adjacent row of poles. At the top of the poles is a horizontal, wire netting that caps the entire assemblage. Vines grow up the wires and snake to some extent along the network on top to produce a thicket by harvest time.

Regional specialties of Lublin include *pieróg gryczany,* also called *pieróg lubelski,* which is a loaf of buckwheat groats, cheese and potatoes baked in dough; and *biały barszcz,* a tart soup made of fermented rye bread with slices of sausage and hard-boiled egg. It is a traditional Easter dish.

Two specialties of the region of Małopolska near Rzeszów deserve special mention. *Zapiekanka z kiełbasą i kartoflami* is a casserole with sour cream, onions and hard-cooked eggs between layers of sausage and potatoes. *Polewka z serwatki* is a cheese soup made with whey and fresh cheese curds, served with potatoes.

## Śląsk (Silesia)

Śląsk, the southwestern region of Poland, has three different geographical sections. Górny Śląsk (Upper Silesia), comprising the eastern, upland portion, is Poland's largest industrial district. The area's largest city, Katowice, is at the district's center. Dolny Śląsk (Lower Silesia), the northwestern portion, is a fertile, lowland farming area along the Odra River. Wrocław is its major city. The most picturesque area of Silesia is the Sudeten Mountains and their foothills, which run along the southwestern edge of the region.

Silesia was a part of ancient Poland from the 900s to 1339, at which time the area came under Bohemian control. It later belonged to Austria (1526) and then, for the most part, to Prussia (1740). After World War I, a portion of Silesia was included in independent Poland. Much of the remainder was incorporated into Poland at the end of World War II. The German residents fled to Germany and Poles expelled from the formerly Polish areas in the east moved to Silesia.

Additions to the menu from Śląsk include *wieprzowina z gruszkami,* pork with pears, and *kluski śląskie,* dumplings made with mashed potatoes and potato flour. They have a central dimple in them made with a finger. The city of Żywiec lies in a valley of the Silesian Beskid Mountains, part of the Carpathian Mountain system. It is known for its brewery and the dishes of *żurek stryszewski,* sour soup made with wheat, *jadło drwali,* two hefty potato pancakes with goulash sandwiched between them, and *żagielek z ryby,* cucumber stuffed with fish.

## Pomorze *(Pomerania) and Kujawy (Kujavia)*

Pomorze, Poland's window on the maritime world, lies in northwestern Poland along the Baltic Sea between the Odra and Vistula Rivers, and is divided into western and eastern portions. It is bordered on the south by the Noteć and Warta River valleys. Its interior is studded with lakes that are well stocked with bass and trout. Grain (especially rye), potatoes and fodder crops such as hay are grown here. The rich soil of the Vistula River valley produces excellent crops of wheat and sugar beets. Among the fish caught in the Baltic Sea are flounder, herring, salmon, cod and eel. Smoked eel is a special favorite. Western Pomerania, the land between the Odra and Łeba Rivers, was a part of ancient Poland from the 10th to the 12th centuries, when it came under German control and remained so aligned for much of its existence. The port city of Szczecin, situated at the mouth of the Odra River is the major urban area in northwestern Poland. Eastern Pomerania includes the port city of Gdańsk (Danzig in German) at the estuary of the Vistula River. Gdańsk is the largest city in the northern part of the country. Another important urban center in Eastern Pomerania is Toruń about 100 miles south of Gdańsk along the Vistula River. Eastern Pomerania has also been under German influence, especially from the Germanic Teutonic Order of Knights, a religious military order.

At the end of World War I, Pomerania remained in Germany, but most of it was incorporated into Poland at the close of World War II. A population exchange followed as the Germans fled and Poles moved in from the formerly Polish regions in the east.

Within Eastern Pomerania is a small wedge of land bordering on the Baltic Sea southwest of Gdańsk called Kaszuby (Kashubia), which is the home of the Kashubian people, descendents of one of the ancient Slavic tribes who peopled this area a millenium ago. Despite their exposure to many other cultures, they assimilated little and most still maintain their folkways and their dialect, which is similar to Polish. Fishing and beekeeping have always been important to their way of life.

The small region of Kujawy (Kujavia) around the Noteć River, bordered on the north by Pomerania and to the south by Great Poland, was a part of the consolidated Polish nation in the 14th century. It was occupied by Prussia after the Second Partition (1793) and returned to independent Poland at the close of World War I.

Herring is frequent fare on Kashubian menus. It is prepared many ways: with cream or vinegar, coated with batter or smoked. Herring in cream often is served with boiled potatoes in jackets (skins)—*kartofle w mundurkach*. Another regional specialty is *śledź po kociewsku,* herring fillet roll-ups filled with mushrooms, onions and pickles in tomato sauce. Also popular is *lin,* a small panfish of the minnow family, called tench. Other regional dishes are *geś po kaszubsku,* Kashubian-style goose cooked in pickle juice with potatoes and rutabaga, flavored with dill and allspice; *zylc,* pig's trotters in aspic; and *panas kaszubski,* Kashubian head cheese.

Specialties of Gdańsk are *kaczka gdańska,* roast duck with oranges served with a baked apple stuffed with red cabbage, and *sola po gdańsku w sosie z krewetek,* sole in shrimp sauce. Other regional offerings are *jajecznica bosmańska,* scrambled eggs with a steak wrapped around a mixture of mushrooms and chopped parsley to form a ball, which is then coated with small croutons, and *kotlet bozmański,* minced meat wrapped around a mixture of mushrooms, breadcrumbs and parsley to form a ball, which is coated with small croutons and deep-fried. (See recipe, p. 51.) Goldwasser, a clear, sweet liqueur containing flecks of gold, has been made in Gdańsk since the late 1500s. Toruń has been famous since medieval times for its honey-spice cake, or gingerbread, called either *miodownick* or *piernik.* Steamed dumplings called *pampuchy* are regional favorites of Szczecin.

## Mazowsze (Mazovia) and Podlasie

Mazowsze lies in the predominantly flat, east central plain of Poland between the Warta and Vistula Rivers. Its soil is not particularly suitable for agriculture, and the region is among the country's poorest. As the Duchy of Mazovia, it existed as an independent branch of the Piast dynasty until it was incorporated into Poland in 1529. Warsaw, the seat of the Mazovian dukes, became the nation's capital in 1569. Poland's second largest metropolis, Łódź, is in western Mazovia. As a result of the Third Partition (1795), Mazovia was occupied jointly by Prussia and Austria, but came under Russian control in 1815. At the close of World War I, Mazovia became a part of independent Poland.

Along the Narew River and its tributaries in the northern reach of Mazovia is an area called Kurpie in the heart of the White Forest (Puszcza Białe) and Green Forest (Puszcza Zielona). The local culture, also named Kurpie, is famous for the traditional carvings over the windows and doorways of the peoples' wooden houses, the intricate art of paper cutting, and Easter palms made of long, wooden poles decorated with flowers and greenery. Historically, the Kurpie provided honey for the kings in exchange for the privilege of hunting and foraging in the royal forests. The hives they tended were hollowed-out cavities high up in the trees. Honey made by wild forest bees is a regional specialty that is featured at an annual honey harvest festival. Traditional regional Kurpie foods include bread and other goods made with honey; smoked and salted pork and goose breast, smoked herring, and *gąski,* green-capped mushrooms native to the area. Honey beer is also available.

Ceramic plate with traditional Kashubian floral pattern featuring stylized tulips.

Menu items include *rosól z zielonki gąski,* broth with green-capped mushrooms, and *jajecznica na solonej gęsinie,* scrambled eggs with salt-cured goose. Another Kurpie specialty is *gołąbki po kurpiowsku,* Kurpie-style cabbage rolls filled with buckwheat groats, diced chicken, and finely chopped hard-boiled eggs.

The cuisine of Warsaw includes a tasty preparation of smoked ham baked in a wrapping of rolled rye-flour dough, which is removed with the skin before serving. Other specialties of Warsaw include *flaczki po warszawsku,* Warsaw-style tripe and vegetables in cream sauce, seasoned with nutmeg, marjoram and ginger, and *sałatka warszawska,* a Warsaw-style salad of beets, beans, peas, pickles and crabmeat in a mayonnaise, sour cream and mustard dressing.

Podlasie is the region northeast of Mazovia, which includes the vast Białowieża primeval forest. Much of the forest escaped the plow and saw because it was a private hunting preserve of Polish kings and rulers of other countries when the area was in their domain. This lowland forest covers about 500 square miles; a small part of it is a Polish national park. Several hundred European bison and numerous other wild animals including wild boars roam the forest. Białystok is the region's largest city. The area was under Prussian domain after the Partitions, and was Russian territory after 1807. It became part of independent Poland after World War I.

Regional dishes include *placki ziemniaczane po mazowiecku,* Mazovian-style potato pancakes with sour cream. The aromatic grass (*trawa żubrowa*) that the bison favor, which is used to flavor a vodka specialty (*żubrówka*), comes from here.

## Mazury (Masuria) and Warmia

Mazury and Warmia lie north of Kurpie, in the northeastern corner of Poland and extend from the Vistula valley in the west to the Soviet border in the north and east. The most prominent city is Olsztyn, in Warmia. Both areas are well covered with forests, and Mazury has several thousand lakes, many interlinked with canals and rivers, with plenty of fish to delight anglers: perch, salmon, bream, and European catfish and whitefish. The countryside around the city of Sulwałki is a tobacco-growing area.

Warmia was wrested from the Teutonic Order of Knights and joined to Poland in 1466. Masuria remained in the Knights' possession as Ducal Prussia. In the First Partition, Warmia was absorbed by Prussia and did not become a part of Poland, nor did Masuria, until after World War II. Poles displaced from the east moved here at that time. A popular fish in Mazuria is *lin*, a small panfish of the minnow family called tench. The area also features *marchew po mazursku*, Masur-style carrots cooked in a cream sauce flavored with dill, and *okoń po mazursku*, perch baked in bacon.

## Foods from Formerly Polish Lands

Several preparations from regions that once were a part of Poland will be encountered on menus. *Barszcz ukraiński* is Ukrainian beet soup with sour cream and vegetables. Typical vegetables added to the beets are potatoes, savoy cabbage, tomatoes and navy beans. Ukraine, or Red Ruthenia, was once a part of the Lithuanian/Polish Empire. *Kołduny* are small, round or semicircular pastas filled with either mutton and suet, or mushrooms, which are boiled and served in soup. *Kołduny* is the Lithuanian name for *pierogi*. The dish is also called *kołduny litewskie*, meaning Lithuanian-style *kołduny*. Lithuanian dishes have become part of the Polish culinary repertoire as a result of the 400-year Polish-Lithuanian union that began in the late 14th century. *Babka podolska* is Podolian-style *babka* with plums. Podole, once in eastern Poland, was incorporated into the Soviet Union after World War II. It is a notable plum-growing area. Dishes from Lwów will be encountered in the Silesian city of Wrocław. The city of Lwów, now L'viv, was also in eastern Poland before it was incorporated into the Soviet Union after World War II. Most of the expelled Poles settled in Wrocław. Some dishes to sample are *flaczki po lwowsku*, Lwów-style broth-based tripe soup with carrots and meat, flavored with caraway; and *naleśniki po lwowsku*, Lwów-style crêpes stuffed with a seasoned potato mixture. (See color insert, p. 8.) *Nugat lwowski*, Lwów-style nougat, is a layer of nougat sandwiched between wafer sheets. A type of *pierogi* originating long ago in the eastern Polish borderlands (Ruthenia) is *pierogi ruskie*, also called *pierogi z kartoflami i serem*. The pastas are filled with a mixture of cheese and potatoes.

### Holiday foods

Many of Poland's folk customs survive today because they have been successfully passed down from one generation to another, despite urbanization and associated changes in lifestyle, and heinous attempts by some nations to eradicate them. Poles are religious—about 95% of the population is Catholic—and their festivals and holidays are tightly interwoven with the Church. The time-honored traditions of the "old world" are observed by Poles around the globe.

Many Poles consider Easter their most important holiday. The preparation for its celebration takes days. Traditional foods need to be readied for Święcone, the blessing of the Easter meal. On the day before Easter, Holy Saturday, families bring a basket of food to church for consecration by the parish priest. The foods are a sampling of what will be eaten on Easter, and include butter or sugar shaped into a lamb, a special round Easter bread decorated with a cross, Polish sausage, ham, smoked bacon, cheese, horseradish, salt and hard-boiled eggs. All items have symbolic meaning, but none is more important than the egg, the symbol of life and the resurrection. The importance of the egg is also evident in the tradition of decorating them for this holiday.

Everyone eagerly anticipates the Easter meal following morning mass, because they have been fasting for the six weeks of Lent. The meal of predominantly cold foods begins with the sharing of the consecrated hard-boiled egg. The egg is cut into pieces, and all gathered around the table wish each other happiness as they share it. The repast that follows includes a beet

*Pisanki drewniany,* wooden Easter eggs with traditional designs burned into them. Polish Easter customs include taking foods that will be be eaten on Easter Sunday to church to be blessed the Saturday before. The egg, symbol of life, is the first of these blessed foods to be eaten.

and horseradish relish (*ćwikła*), patês, sausages, ham and several Polish Easter cake specialties. There is a tall sweet yeast cake (*babka wielkanocna*) containing citron, candied orange and lemon peel, raisins and almonds, which is decorated with icing or baker's confetti; several types of rectangular flat cakes (*mazurek,* singular) with crusts of flaky dough or wafer sheets typically topped with nut or fruit mixtures that are richly decorated; and cheesecake (*sernik*) made with farmer's cheese.

Another holiday very important to Poles is the day before Christmas. On Christmas Eve families gather for a special meatless dinner called *wigilia.* According to tradition, this is a fasting day and one cannot eat until the evening star, the Star of Bethlehem, is sighted. Custom requires the evening's feast to have an odd number of courses. The traditional number is thirteen, which represents the 12 apostles and Christ. Not every family can afford such an elaborate dinner, however, and the number of odd dishes is reduced in keeping with the wealth and size of the household. Several superstitious beliefs dictate that an even number of diners be seated at the table, and it was customary to invite a guest, or even a stranger, to ensure a round number.

Thin baked wafers (*opłatki*) made of fine wheat flour are shared as the first food of the meal. All family and friends assembled at a household are given a wafer. The sharing ceremony begins with the host and hostess breaking off and eating a piece of each other's wafer while at the same time extending wishes of happiness in the year ahead. Everyone then participates in the ceremony until all have exchanged blessings (and sometimes mutual forgiveness) in a similar manner. All subsequently sit down to partake of the special holiday dishes.

There are several customary preparations one can expect to find on the table. Among them are *barszcz z uszkami,* a clear beet soup with tiny pasta squares that have been folded over a mushroom filling to form a triangle and pinched together at two ends. Since it traditionally is a part of the Christmas Eve supper (*wigilia*) it is named *barszcz czysty wigilijny.* There are also likely to be *kluski z makiem i rodzynkami,* a dish of poppy seed noodles, *kompot wigilijny z dwunastu owoców,* a compote containing 12 dried fruits, and *pierogi.* Fish dishes include *śledź w oleju,* herring in oil, and *karp po żydowsku,* Jewish-style poached carp steaks cooked in a caramel sauce with raisins, cloves and almonds. Desserts include *makowiec,* which has a filling of finely ground poppy seeds mixed with honey, raisins, nuts and vanilla. The filling is spread on yeast dough and the dough is then rolled up into a jelly roll. An interesting menu item of special importance in southeastern Poland is *kutia wigilijna,* a sweet, cold, vanilla-flavored dish of boiled wheat with honey, poppy seeds and raisins. In some families a spoonful of the mixture traditionally was tossed onto the ceiling. The number of wheat grains that adhered was said to predict the size of the grain harvest in the coming year.

A Christmas wafer (*opłatek*) imprinted with a religious image. The breaking and sharing of wafers, with its accompanying exchange of good wishes, is the most important ceremony on Christmas eve.

# Tastes of Poland

You are encouraged to try some of these classic and nouvelle Polish recipes before you leave home. This is a wonderful and immediately rewarding way to preview the extraordinary cuisine of Poland. Most of the special Polish ingredients necessary for these recipes are available in the United States (see *Resources,* p. 65). Satisfactory substitutes are given for unavailable ones.

## APPETIZERS

### Śledź Tatarski z Majerankiem

*Herring tartare flavored with marjoram.* Serves 8.

This recipe was provided by Bernard Lussiana, executive head chef of Warsaw's Hotel Le Royal Meridien Bristol. Chef Lussiana weaves traditional Polish foods into exquisite new combinations.

*Tartare*

1 POUND MARINATED HERRING

2 TEASPOONS SHALLOTS, CHOPPED VERY THIN

2 TABLESPOONS MARINATED GHERKINS, CUT IN ⅛ -INCH DICE

2 TABLESPOONS FRESH MARJORAM, CHOPPED

4 TABLESPOONS VIRGIN OLIVE OIL

2 TEASPOONS TOMATO PASTE

½ TEASPOON DIJON MUSTARD

2 TABLESPOONS FRESH LEMON JUICE

SALT AND PEPPER TO TASTE

*Lettuce salad*

⅔ POUND LAMB'S LETTUCE, WASHED*

4½ TABLESPOONS VIRGIN OLIVE OIL

4 TEASPOONS HAZELNUT OIL

[Śledź Tatarski z Majerankiem, *continued*]

> 2 TEASPOONS FRESH LEMON JUICE
>
> 1 TEASPOON DIJON MUSTARD
>
> SALT AND PEPPER TO TASTE
>
> *Garnish*
>
> FRESH DILL
>
> FRESH MARJORAM
>
> 8 SLICES BREAD FOR TOAST (OPTIONAL)
>
> 8 QUAIL EGGS (OPTIONAL)†
>
> 1½ OUNCES SALMON CAVIAR (OPTIONAL)

Rinse herring under fresh water, dry and chop coarsely in about ¼-inch dice. Add shallots, gherkins, marjoram, tomato paste and mustard. Mix in olive oil and lemon juice. Add salt and pepper to taste and set aside in refrigerator.

Prepare the salad dressing and set aside. Gently open the quail eggs and keep in their shells. With a round cutter about 3 inches in diameter, form the tartare on a chilled plate. If desired, garnish on top with an opened, raw quail egg in the shell. Put a crown of lamb's lettuce around the tartare, sprinkle with dressing and a touch of salmon caviar. Decorate with fresh dill and marjoram and serve immediately with warm toast on the side.

\**Valerianella olitoria.* The leaves of this herb are oval to round, and are used in salads and as herbs. It is not cultivated to any extent in the United States, so substitute a lettuce of your choice.

†See *Resources* (p. 65) for mail-order suppliers. Also, some university poultry departments have quail eggs. If you are near a campus, inquire there.

## Bigos

*Hunter's stew.* Serves 10–12.

Roma Górnicka, editor of the popular Polish gourmet food magazine *Kuchnia,* contributed the recipe for this hearty stew. Traditionally served as a hot appetizer, it also can be a main dish.

> 4 OUNCES DRIED, WILD MUSHROOMS (PREFERABLY *BOLETUS EDULIS,*
>
>   THE KING BOLETE OR *PORCINI* MUSHROOM)
>
> 3 POUNDS BONE-IN MEAT: PORK, BEEF ROAST
>
>   AND ¼ DUCK
>
> 5 OUNCES (1 CUP) RED ONIONS, FINELY SLICED
>
> 3–4 JUNIPER BERRIES

12 BLACK PEPPERCORNS

3–4 WHOLE ALLSPICE BERRIES

1 BAY LEAF

1–2 CLOVES

SALT TO TASTE

1 POUND GREEN CABBAGE, FINELY SHREDDED

4 POUNDS SAUERKRAUT (NOT TOO SOUR), CHOPPED

1 POUND SMOKED POLISH PORK SAUSAGE (*KIEłBASA*)

4 OUNCES SMOKED LEAN BACON

3 TABLESPOONS PRUNES, SLICED

3 TABLESPOONS RAISINS, SLICED

1 TABLESPOON MUSTARD

3 OUNCES TOMATO PASTE

⅔ CUP MADEIRA, PORTO OR DRY RED WINE

Rinse mushrooms and soak in water for 2–3 hours. Drain and cut into slices. Set aside. Stew meat (pork, beef and duck) for 1 hour in 3 cups water with onions, juniper berries, peppercorns, allspice, bay leaf, cloves and salt to taste. Put cabbage in boiling water to blanch it and continue to boil until half tender, about 15 minutes. Drain and set aside. In 6- or 8-quart pot, cook sauerkraut in a little water for one hour, stirring occasionally. Add more water if necessary. Stir in cabbage and mushrooms. Remove cooked meat from bones and cut into 1-inch cubes. Add to mixture, together with stewing broth and spices. Cut sausage into small pieces and stir in. Continue simmering on low heat about 2 more hours, uncovered, stirring often so sauerkraut doesn't burn. Fry bacon, crumble and add to pot. Continue cooking until most of the liquid has evaporated, stirring constantly. Add prunes, raisins, mustard, tomato paste and wine, Madeira or Porto. Cook 15–20 minutes longer, stirring occasionally. Serve with hard-crust rye bread.

### Jaja Faszerowane na Gorąco

*Hot stuffed eggs Polonaise.* Serves 4–6.

This recipe for a universally applauded Polish speciality was contributed by Robert and Maria Strybel, who live in Warsaw, the capital of Poland. They have written the delightful and definitive Polish cookbook in English, *Polish Heritage Cookery*.

6 EGGS

2 TABLESPOONS BUTTER

1–2 ONIONS, FINELY CHOPPED

[Jaja Faszerowane na Gorąco, *continued*]

> 1 EGG (OR 1 TABLESPOON SOUR CREAM)
>
> SALT AND PEPPER TO TASTE
>
> 2–3 TABLESPOONS DILL, CHOPPED VERY FINE
>
> 2–3 TABLESPOONS CHIVES, CHOPPED (OPTIONAL)
>
> BREADCRUMBS
>
> BUTTER

Cook 6 very fresh eggs in boiling water until hard boiled; then cool in cold water. When eggs are at room temperature, wipe dry. Take one egg at a time and position it firmly on a cutting board. Using a heavy, sharp knife with a non-serrated edge tap each egg lengthwise and quickly cut through with a slight back and forth motion all the way to the cutting board, shell and all. With a small spoon carefully scoop out the cooked white and yolk of each egg, taking care not to damage the shell. Remove any shell fragments that adhere to the eggs. Gently remove and discard any jagged shell splinters around the rims of shells and set shell halves aside.

Sauté onions in butter until golden and tender. Combine onions with eggs and grind or chop very fine. Stir in 1 raw beaten egg (or sour cream), and season mixture to taste with salt, pepper and dill. Mix well. Chopped chives may also be added if desired. If mixture appears too soft, firm it up by stirring in a tablespoon or so of breadcrumbs and mixing well. Fill egg shells with mixture until slightly mounded, and gently press mixture into shell. When ready to serve, dip filling side of shell halves in breadcrumbs and sauté in hot butter. They are ready when a golden-brown crust forms on filling and tops of shells are very hot to the touch. Serve at once.

## SOUPS & ACCOMPANIMENTS

### Zupa Ogórkowa

*Dill pickle soup.* Serves 8–10.

This recipe was provided by Ela and Andy Wasielewski, co-owners of Crocus, a Polish restaurant in Milwaukee, Wisconsin. Both are from that part of Poland called Mazovia: Ela is from Warsaw, Poland's capital, and Andy is from Łódź.

> 1 POUND BEEF NECK BONES
>
> 3 QUARTS WATER
>
> ½ CUP CARROTS, SHREDDED
>
> ½ CUP CELERY, DICED
>
> 1½ CUP RAW POTATOES, CUT INTO ½-INCH DICE
>
> 1 POUND BRINE-CURED DILL PICKLES, COARSELY SHREDDED

SALT TO TASTE

½ CUP FLOUR

1 CUP WATER

FRESH DILL FOR GARNISH

Place bones in pot with water. Bring to a boil, then reduce heat and cook 1 hour. Remove scum on surface. Discard neck bones and strain broth. Add carrots, celery and potatoes to the strained broth, and simmer for 15 minutes. Add pickles and simmer an additional ½ hour. Potatoes should be tender. Add salt to taste. Blend flour with water until lump-free. Add enough to simmering soup to lightly thicken it. The amount added will vary, depending on how much water evaporated while making the beef stock. Serve with fresh dill sprinkled on top.

## Barszcz Czysty Wigilijny

*Clear beet soup for Christmas Eve.* Serves 8–10.

Roma Górnicka, editor of the popular Polish gourmet food magazine *Kuchnia,* contributed the recipe for this classic soup made for *wigilia,* the traditional dinner on Christmas Eve.

3 POUNDS BEETS (9 AT ABOUT 5–6 OUNCES EACH)

10 OUNCES CARROTS

7 OUNCES PARSLEY ROOT

4 OUNCES CELERIAC ROOT

1 MEDIUM LEEK

1 MEDIUM ONION

6–8 DRIED, WILD MUSHROOMS (PREFERABLY *BOLETUS EDULIS,*
    THE KING BOLETE OR *PORCINI* MUSHROOM)

10 BLACK PEPPERCORNS

2–3 WHOLE ALLSPICE BERRIES

1 SMALL BAY LEAF

1 CUP DRY RED WINE

1 TEASPOON SALT, OR TO TASTE

LEMON JUICE TO TASTE OR

    1–2 TEASPOONS *BARSZCZ CZERWONY*\* (BEET SOUR)

SUGAR TO TASTE

[Barszcz Czysty Wigilijny, *continued*]

    1 CLOVE GARLIC, MINCED (OPTIONAL)

    8–10 EGGS, HARD-BOILED

Rinse mushrooms thoroughly and soak in water for 2–3 hours, then simmer until tender. Drain, reserving broth. The mushrooms can be used for miniature, mushroom-filled pastas (*uszka*) traditionally served with this soup on Christmas Eve (recipe not included) or saved for another use. Peel 2 beets, carrots, parsley root and celeriac, rinse and cut into large pieces. Quarter onion and cut leek into 2-inch pieces. Place vegetables in a large pot and cover with 8 cups water. Add spices, bring to a boil and cook 40–50 minutes. Strain, reserving stock. Wash remaining beets, saving one for making juice, and cook unpeeled until tender. Drain, cool, peel and grate beets, and add to vegetable stock. Add mushroom stock. Heat soup but do not boil. Season with lemon juice or beet sour, salt, sugar and red wine. Finely grate reserved beet and squeeze juice out of gratings. Add to soup. Shortly before serving soup, add 1 minced garlic clove for seasoning, if desired. Serve with (*uszka*) or with a hard-boiled egg cut in half or quarters.

*Available at markets carrying Polish foods; also see *Resources* (p. 65) for mail-order suppliers.

### Rosół z Wołowiny, Kury lub Grzybów z Kluskami Lanemi

*Beef, chicken or mushroom broth with egg-drop noodles.* Serves 2–4.

This recipe was provided by Zofia Kubinski, who is originally from Kielce, a city in the southeastern region of Poland called Małopolska (Little Poland). She now lives in the United States.

    *Broth*

    2 POUNDS BEEF SHANK OR CHICKEN, OR 2 OUNCES DRIED WILD

        MUSHROOMS (PREFERABLY THE KING BOLETE OR *PORCINI* MUSHROOM)*†

    1–2 QUARTS WATER

    5 PEPPERCORNS

    1 BAY LEAF

    1 MEDIUM CARROT, QUARTERED

    1 ONION, QUARTERED

    5 SPRIGS PARSLEY

    ½ TEASPOON SALT

    1 TABLESPOON BEEF OR CHICKEN BOUILLON GRANULES

*Noodles*

1 EGG

4 TABLESPOONS FLOUR

1–2 TEASPOONS WATER

¼ TEASPOON SALT

FRESH PARSLEY FOR GARNISH, FINELY CHOPPED (OPTIONAL)

To make broth, bring beef, chicken or mushrooms to boil in water, then reduce heat and skim scum from the surface. Add peppercorns and bay leaf, and simmer, covered, about 1 hour. Add carrot, onion, parsley, salt and bouillon, and simmer another hour. Strain broth and set aside. Reserve meat for another use. To make noodles, have ready a pot of simmering water. In a small bowl, beat egg with flour, water and salt until smooth. Slowly pour a thin stream of batter into gently simmering water. Cook for 1 minute, then drain in a colander. To serve, put noodles in a serving dish or individual soup bowls, and pour broth over them. Garnish with parsley if desired.

*A little light cream can be added to the cooked mushroom broth if desired.

†Available at markets carrying Polish foods; also see *Resources* (p. 65) for mail-order suppliers.

## Pulpety Nadziewane Jajkami Przepiórki w Zurku

*Meatballs stuffed with quail eggs in* żurek *(white borscht), a sour ryemeal soup.*
Serves 6–8.

This recipe was provided by Maciej Kuroń, owner and chef of the Studio Buffo restaurant in Warsaw. Mr. Kuroń, the most popular culinary personality on Polish television, has a show called "Let's Cook with Mr. Kuroń."

*Sour ryemeal (make 3–4 days ahead)*

4 CUPS WATER

1 CUP RYE FLOUR

CRUST FROM SLICE OF RYE BREAD

4 SMALL GARLIC CLOVES, MINCED

*Soup stock*

6 CUPS WATER

½ TEASPOON DRIED MARJORAM

¼ TEASPOON THYME

½ TEASPOON CARAWAY SEEDS

[Pulpety Nadziewane Jajkami Przepiórki w Zurku, *continued*]

1 BAY LEAF

TEASPOONS VEGETABLE BASE*

SALT AND PEPPER TO TASTE

3–4 DRIED WILD MUSHROOMS (KING BOLETE OR *PORCINI* MUSHROOM)

2 CUPS SOUR RYEMEAL (SEE ABOVE)

1 CUP HEAVY CREAM

*Meatballs*

12 QUAIL EGGS*

1 SMALL ONION, CHOPPED

VEGETABLE OIL

¾ POUND MINCED MEAT (HALF VEAL, HALF PORK)

½ TEASPOON DRIED MARJORAM

2 SMALL CLOVES GARLIC, MINCED

¾ TEASPOON SALT

¼ TEASPOON PEPPER

*Garnish*

FRESH DILL, CHOPPED

To make sour ryemeal mixture, boil water and cool to lukewarm. Put one cup lukewarm water into glass or ceramic bowl. Add rye flour and blend well. Add remaining water, bread crust and garlic. Mix together, cover bowl with towel and set aside in a warm place (75°–80°F) for 3–4 days. The mixture will bubble. Strain mixture through cheesecloth into a jar. Tightly cover and refrigerate the unused portion. It can be reserved for several weeks for another batch of soup.

To make soup stock, put water in large saucepan. Add herbs, vegetable base, and salt and pepper to taste. Bring to boiling and simmer for 20 minutes. Cover mushrooms with boiling water and set aside to soften.

Gently hard boil quail eggs in lightly salted water until done, about 3 minutes. Run under cold water, drain, remove shells and set aside.

To make meatballs, fry onion in a little vegetable oil until golden. Drain and add to minced meat. Add herbs, garlic, and salt and pepper. Mix well. Divide into 12 balls. Poke a hole in each ball and gently place an egg in the center. Press meat around egg to completely enclose it and roll meatball in palms of the hand to distribute meat uniformly around egg. Return soup to burner and bring to simmering. Put meatballs in soup and gently simmer for 20 minutes. Remove with slotted spoon, set aside and keep warm. Strain soup, return to saucepan and continue simmering. Cut mushrooms into strips and add them to the soup, along with the water they were soaked in. Stir sour ryemeal mixture well and add 2 cups of it to soup. Add cream

and mix well. To serve, cut meatballs in half and place in soup bowls. Add soup and garnish with dill.
*See *Resources* (p. 65) for mail-order suppliers.

## Polewka z Serwatki
*Soup (gruel) made with whey.* Serves 8.
Emilia Bałajewicz, who lives in the small village of Baryczka near Rzeszów in south-eastern Poland, provided this recipe. The soup, without the addition of cheese curds, is also a great starter for cream-based soups.

½ GALLON WHOLE MILK

½ CUP FLOUR

¾ CUP WHOLE MILK

⅔ CUP SOUR CREAM

SALT TO TASTE (OPTIONAL)

Put ½ gallon whole milk in a bowl that has been rinsed with scalding water, cover with cloth and set aside at room temperature 3 days to sour. Transfer soured milk to a pan and bring to a boil. Strain curds from whey and set aside. Return whey to pan and bring to a boil. In a separate container, blend flour with ¾ cup whole milk, gradually adding more milk and stirring continuously to form a smooth mixture. Slowly add to whey. For a thinner soup, add less milk/flour mixture to whey. Slowly blend in sour cream with a whisk. Add some crumbled cheese curds to the soup and serve with potatoes.

## Zupa Szczawiowa
*Sorrel soup.* Serves 6–8.
This recipe was contributed by Judy Krauza, who leads the Folk Crafts Tour to Poland for Craft World Tours in Byron, New York.

6 CUPS MEAT STOCK

½ POUND SORREL

1½–2 CUPS RAW POTATOES, DICED

4 TABLESPOONS FLOUR

2 CUPS WHOLE MILK

FRESH YOUNG DILL (OR PARSLEY), CHOPPED

1 HARD-BOILED EGG, CUT IN HALF, SLICED OR CHOPPED (OPTIONAL)

[Zupa Szczawiowa, *continued*]
Bring stock to a boil. Remove sorrel leaves from stems and chop leaves very fine in a food processor. Add processed leaves and potatoes to boiling water. Simmer covered for 15 minutes. Whisk flour into milk and stir into simmering soup. Continue simmering for at least 5 minutes until raw flour taste is gone. Place some hard-boiled egg in each serving dish, as desired, and add soup. Garnish with dill or parsley.

## Zupa Jagodowa

*Blueberry soup.* Serves 4–6.
The recipe for this soup was provided by Wanda Sicińska, who is from Warsaw. Dr. Sicińska is a research associate in the Institute of Organic Chemistry at the Polish Academy of Sciences.

1 QUART FRESH BLUEBERRIES

SUGAR TO TASTE

CINNAMON TO TASTE

¼ CUP WATER

1½ TABLESPOON FLOUR

COOKED NOODLES (OPTIONAL)

Rinse blueberries and set 1½ cup aside. In saucepan, pour one quart hot water over remaining blueberries and cook for about five minutes. Add sugar and cinnamon to taste. Slowly mix water into flour. Stir until lump-free and add to simmering soup. Simmer for one minute. Remove from heat and set aside. Coarsely mash uncooked blueberries and add to soup. Serve warm or cold over noodles.

## Łatwe Paszteciki

*Easy soup pastries.* Serves many.
Robert and Maria Strybel, co-authors of *Polish Heritage Cookery,* provide the easiest way to make these soup accompaniments: savory fillings wrapped in a pastry crust. Robert Strybel, using the byline "The Polish Chef," writes a column about Polish food for several Polish-American newspapers.

2 8-OUNCE PACKAGES (TUBES) OF REFRIGERATOR CRESCENT ROLL DOUGH

*Meat filling*

¾ POUNDS COOKED BEEF AND/OR PORK

1–2 SMALL ONIONS, FINELY CHOPPED

BUTTER

1 EGG

1 TABLESPOON BREADCRUMBS

SALT AND PEPPER TO TASTE

PINCH GARLIC POWDER AND/OR MARJORAM (OPTIONAL)

*Mushroom filling*

12 OUNCES MUSHROOMS, FRESHLY SLICED

1 MEDIUM ONION, COARSELY CHOPPED

3 TABLESPOONS FAT

1 EGG

2 TABLESPOONS BREADCRUMBS

SALT AND PEPPER TO TASTE

2 TEASPOONS FRESH DILL AND/OR PARSLEY, CHOPPED

Break open tubes of refrigerator dough and spread dough out on lightly floured board or kitchen counter. Dip fingers in flour and press down on manufacturer's perforations to obliterate them. Cut each dough sheet lengthwise into two equal strips. Run filling of choice down center of strips and fold dough over it. Pinch to seal edges. Cut at an angle into 2- or 2½-inch pieces and bake according to directions on package. Serve as a hot, hand-held accompaniment to clear soups (beet, tomato), bouillon or consommé.

To make meat filling, grind together beef and/or pork with onions sautéed in a little butter. Add egg and breadcrumbs, and mix well by hand. Season to taste with salt, pepper and, if desired, garlic powder and/or marjoram. Provides enough filling for all four strips of dough.

To make mushroom stuffing, sauté mushrooms and onions in fat on medium-high heat, stirring frequently, until fully cooked. The mushrooms and onions should be tender, all moisture should evaporate and the mushrooms should begin to sizzle. When cool enough to handle, grind. Stir in egg and breadcrumbs and season with salt, pepper and chopped dill and/or parsley. Provides enough filling for all four strips of dough.

# SALADS

## Sałatka Szefa Kuchni

*Chef's special house salad.* Serves 10.

This recipe was provided by Zbigniew Sekuła (pictured on the front cover), executive chef of the Wierzynek Restaurant in Cracow. This venerable eating establishment has a history of hospitality and fine foods since 1364.

4 POUNDS SMOKED CHICKEN

1¾ POUNDS GRAPES

[Sałatka Szefa Kuchni, *continued*]

    2 CUPS CASHEWS

    ¾ CUP MAYONNAISE

    ¾ CUP PLAIN YOGURT

    ½ CUP HONEY

    WHITE OR BLACK PEPPER

    SALT TO TASTE

    *Garnish*

    LETTUCE LEAVES

    LEMON SLICES

    GREEN BELL PEPPER SLICES

    FRESH PARSLEY

    CUCUMBER SLICES

Remove skin from chicken and discard. Bone and cut meat into small cubes and set aside. Combine mayonnaise, yogurt and honey. Add salt and pepper to taste. Mix in chicken, cashews and grapes. If grapes are large, cut in half before adding. Refrigerate for about two hours. Place salad on lettuce leaves and decorate with pieces of pepper, lemon and cucumber slices and some parsley.

## Mizeria

*Cucumber salad.* Serves 4.

The name of this popular salad is derived from the Latin word for misery. It is said that Queen Bona Sforza of Milan, who married the Polish King Zygmunt I in 1518, wept for her homeland when she ate it.

    2 LARGE CUCUMBERS, PEELED

    SALT

    1 CUP SOUR CREAM

    1 TEASPOON SUGAR

    1½ TABLESPOONS FRESHLY SQUEEZED LEMON JUICE

    PEPPER TO TASTE

    1–2 TABLESPOONS FRESH DILL, CHOPPED

Cut cucumbers into very thin slices. Sprinkle generously with salt, toss lightly and set aside for 30 minutes. Drain off liquid. Place slices on paper towels, and pat dry with additional paper towels. Mix sour cream with sugar, lemon juice, pepper and dill. Add cucumbers and stir well. Serve immediately.

## Sałatka z Kartofli

*Potato salad.* Serves 4–6.

This recipe was contributed by Jurek (George) and Aleksandra Burzynski, co-owners of Polonez, a Polish restaurant in Milwaukee, Wisconsin. Jurek is from Łódź, a city in the region of Poland called Mazovia, and Aleksandra is from Gyndia, a port city on the Baltic, in the region of Poland called Pomerania.

1¼ POUNDS COLD POTATOES, BOILED UNPEELED

¾ CUP COLD COOKED CARROTS, CUT INTO ¼-INCH DICE

¾ CUP COOKED CELERY, FINELY CHOPPED

3–4 TABLESPOONS BRINE-CURED DILL PICKLES, FINELY CHOPPED

2–3 TABLESPOONS ONION, FINELY CHOPPED

MAYONNAISE TO TASTE

4 TEASPOONS SUGAR

SALT AND PEPPER TO TASTE

¼ CUP MILK OR CREAM (OPTIONAL)

Remove skins and cut potatoes into ¼-inch dice (4 cups). Add carrots, celery, pickles and onions, and mix together. Add mayonnaise to consistency desired. Blend in sugar. Add salt and pepper to taste. Milk or cream can be added for a creamier salad.

# MAIN DISHES

## Kotlet Bosmański

*Bosun's cutlet.* Serves 4–6.

This recipe was provided by Roman Groszewski, owner of the Kubicki restaurant in Gdańsk. This port city is the largest in the region of northern Poland called Pomerania.

*Croutons*

4 SMALL, DAY-OLD BREAD ROLLS

*Stuffing*

5 TABLESPOONS BUTTER

2 OUNCES BUTTON MUSHROOMS, FINELY CHOPPED

¾ OUNCE FRESH PARSLEY LEAVES, FINELY CHOPPED

4 OUNCES BREADCRUMBS

*Meatballs*

1 SMALL, DAY-OLD HARD ROLL

¼ CUP MILK

[Kotlet Bosmański, *continued*]

¾ POUND LEAN VEAL

¾ POUND LEAN BEEF

5 LARGE CLOVES GARLIC, MINCED

¾ TEASPOON SALT

PEPPER TO TASTE

2 EGGS

OIL FOR DEEP FRYING STUFFED MEATBALLS

To make croutons, cut four rolls into ⅜-inch cubes, and toast in oven at 350°F until golden brown. Set aside.

To make stuffing, melt butter and add mushrooms, parsley and breadcrumbs. Mix well and refrigerate to solidify butter.

Grind meat two times, using a meat grinder with a small-holed grinding plate (or have your butcher do this). Break fifth roll into small pieces and soak in milk. Add to meat mixture and blend well. Mash garlic with salt and pepper, and add to meat. Add eggs and mix well. Form balls about 2–2½ inches in diameter (about 2½–3 ounces each). To stuff, hold ball in palm and make a deep cavity in it with the thumb. Press sides to make cavity large enough to hold and enclose about 1 tablespoon stuffing. Put stuffing in cavity, roll edges of meat up and over it, and pinch closed. Roll stuffed ball in croutons, and press them well into meat. The surface should be lightly studded with croutons, not completely covered with them. Deep-fry balls in oil on medium-low setting, about 10 minutes, or until brown and completely cooked. Adjust heat if balls brown too fast. Drain on paper towels. The chef suggests serving meatballs with boiled potatoes with hunter's sauce (sauce flavored with juniper berries) or mushroom sauce, or rice, and grated beets with butter or cabbage.

## Kaczka Pieczona z Jabłkami

*Roasted duck with apples.* Serves 4.

Zbigniew Sekuła (pictured on the front cover), executive chef of the Wierzynek restaurant in Cracow, provided this recipe.

1 4-POUND DUCK (WEIGHT NOT INCLUDING GIBLETS AND NECK)

1 TEASPOON SALT

1 TEASPOON FRESH MARJORAM

3 LARGE GRANNY SMITH APPLES, PEELED, CORED AND QUARTERED

2½ TABLESPOONS SUGAR

¼ CUP FREESTONE PEACH SLICES IN SYRUP

1 CUP FRESH CRANBERRIES, WASHED

2 TEASPOONS BUTTER

Prepare duck for roasting by washing body cavity, patting dry and rubbing with salt and marjoram. Roll apples in sugar and place in cavity, sew cavity closed and fasten or bind legs. Add small amount of water to roasting pan, place duck on rack in pan and bake at 350°F 1½–2 hours, or until fork tender. Baste the duck with water first, then with its own juices as they develop during baking. When done, cut the roasted duck into quarters and put on serving dish. Surround duck with apples from the cavity. Sauté cranberries in butter in a small pan for two minutes over low heat. Cranberries will remain whole but will soften. Garnish with peaches and cranberries. The chef suggests serving with potatoes and red cabbage.

## Zrazy

*Beef roll-ups.* Serves 4.

This recipe was provided by Halina Bartowiak, a native of Poznań, the major city of the region of Poland called Wielkopolska (Great Poland).

2¼ POUNDS BEEF RUMP ROAST

DIJON MUSTARD

2 MEDIUM ONIONS, FINELY CHOPPED

4 STRIPS SMOKED BACON (DOUBLE SMOKED IF POSSIBLE), CUT IN HALF
    CROSSWISE

2 MEDIUM BRINED-CURED PICKLES, QUARTERED

PEPPER TO TASTE

SALT

1 TABLESPOON FLOUR

Cut meat against the grain into 8 pieces. With a meat mallet moistened with water, flatten each piece into a ¼-inch thick scallop about 4 inches wide by 8 inches long, and spread mustard on one side. Along one of the shorter ends of each scallop place a pickle strip, ½ strip of bacon and some chopped onion. Roll up meat like a jelly roll and fasten with toothpicks. Give each rolled scallop a light dusting of salt on all sides. Place in frying pan without oil and brown on low heat, turning to cook all sides. Put in a single layer in a casserole dish and add juices from frying pan to a depth of ½ inch. Add water if necessary. Cover and bake in a preheated oven at 350°F for 1½ hours, turning roll-ups once or twice during baking. Remove to warm serving platter and take out toothpicks. To make gravy, put flour in sauce pan and slowly add ¼ cup of the cooking broth. Blend well. Add 1¾ cups more cooking broth (supplement with water, if necessary). If amount of broth remaining in casserole is less than this, add water to it. Simmer over low heat until thickened, stirring as needed. Serve with roll-ups.

## VEGETABLES & SIDE DISHES

### Kalafior po Polsku

*Cauliflower Polonaise.* Serves 6.

Cooked vegetables topped with breadcrumbs browned in butter (Polonaise topping) are a Polish favorite, especially when the vegetable is cauliflower.

> 1 3-POUND HEAD CAULIFLOWER
>
> SALT
>
> 1 TEASPOON SUGAR
>
> 1 TABLESPOON BUTTER
>
> 3 TABLESPOONS BREADCRUMBS

Remove leaves of cauliflower and cut off tough stem. Cover trimmed head in pan of salted boiling water, add sugar and cook, uncovered, until tender, about 25 minutes. Drain and keep warm on serving plate. Melt butter in small saucepan. Add breadcrumbs and lightly brown. Sprinkle breadcrumb mixture on top of cauliflower, whole or cut into sections, and serve.

### Kopytki

*Potato dumplings.* Serves many.

This recipe was provided by Sophie Hodorowicz Knab, who lives in the United States. She is the author of *Polish Customs, Traditions and Folklore; Polish Herbs, Flowers and Folk Medicine* and *Polish Wedding Customs and Traditions.* This is one of Sophie's favorite comfort foods. Her mother often made it out of leftover boiled potatoes.

> 1 CUP FLOUR
>
> ½ TEASPOON SALT
>
> 3 CUPS COOKED POTATOES, RICED OR MASHED
>
> 1 EGG, BEATEN

Bring a pan of lightly salted water to a boil. Place flour in a mound on a large work surface, and sprinkle salt on top of flour. Put mashed or riced potatoes on top of mound of flour. Make a well in the center and add the beaten egg. Work the mixture slowly with the hands. Some water may be needed to work the flour and potatoes together. If so, add slowly, a couple of tablespoons at a time. Knead lightly. The dough should be soft and light. Divide the dough in half, and on a floured surface roll into a long, sausage-shaped strip about ½–1 inch thick. With a sharp knife, cut each strip into ¼-inch thick pieces at an angle. Gently cook in boiling water until they float to the top, within 5–6 minutes. Remove carefully with a slotted spoon and allow to drain briefly in a colander. Place on a well-buttered platter and serve immediately. Do not allow dumplings to overlap one another, as they will stick. They are delicious with leftover gravy of any kind and are a vegetable side dish for a meatless dinner. In Poland, the cooked *kopytki* are drizzled with bacon drippings and bits of bacon.

# DESSERTS

## Sernik

*Cheesecake.* Serves 10–12.

This recipe was provided by Beata Kuczek, an attorney practicing law in Cracow. This major center of Polish culture is located in southeastern Poland in the region called Małopolska.

2½ STICKS BUTTER (10 OUNCES)

3½ CUPS POWDERED SUGAR

10 EGGS

2¼ POUNDS POLISH WHITE FARMER'S CHEESE MADE FROM WHOLE MILK*

¼ TEASPOON SALT

1 TEASPOON BAKING POWDER

1 TEASPOON VANILLA

6 TABLESPOONS FINE-GRAIN DURUM SEMOLINA

4 TABLESPOONS POWDERED SUGAR FOR EGG WHITES

RAISINS (OPTIONAL)

CANDIED ORANGE PEEL, FINELY DICED (OPTIONAL)

Butter bottom and sides of a 10" spring-form pan with 2" sides. Lightly sprinkle buttered surface with breadcrumbs and set aside. In a large bowl, cream butter. Separate egg whites from egg yolks and set aside. Add small amount of powdered sugar to creamed butter, mixing well. Blend in one egg yolk. Continue alternating addition of powdered sugar and egg yolks, beating well between each addition. Grind cheese twice in a food grinder or mix in a processor until smooth and paste-like, being careful not to mix so long that the cheese becomes watery. Add cheese to batter and blend well. Stir in salt, vanilla and baking powder. Add semolina and mix well. If desired, add raisins and candied orange peel to taste. Beat egg whites until frothy. Slowly add powdered sugar and beat until whites are stiff but not dry. Gently fold whites into batter so they retain their loft. Fill spring-form pan with batter. Bake cake on middle rack of preheated oven (350°F) for 1 hour. During baking, cake will rise slightly above top of pan, but will collapse when it cools. Top will be golden brown. Center may be a little soft. As soon as cake is removed from oven, place on serving plate and run a knife around side of pan to loosen it.

[Sernik, *continued*]
Sprinkle top with sifted powdered sugar. Refrigerate cake to cool. Remove pan sides when cake has cooled and set.
*Available at markets selling Polish foods; also see *Resources* (p. 65) for mail-order suppliers.

### Sernik Przekladany

*Layered cheesecake.* Serves many.
This recipe was provided by Bogusława Bogacka, who is from Rzeszów, the major city in southeastern Poland.

*Top and bottom layers*

4¾ CUPS FLOUR

3 TEASPOONS BAKING POWDER

1 CUP BUTTER

2½ CUPS POWDERED SUGAR

7 EGG YOLKS

5 TABLESPOONS VEGETABLE OIL

7 TABLESPOONS SOUR CREAM

4 TEASPOONS COCOA TO COLOR ONE LAYER OF DOUGH

*Middle layer*

2¼ POUNDS POLISH WHITE FARMER'S CHEESE MADE WITH WHOLE MILK

3 CUPS POWDERED SUGAR

4 TEASPOONS BAKING POWDER

5 TABLESPOONS SOUR CREAM

7 EGG WHITES

1 TABLESPOON POWDERED SUGAR FOR EGG WHITES

2 TABLESPOONS POTATO FLOUR

1 TABLESPOON REGULAR FLOUR

LEMON JUICE OR DICED, CANDIED ORANGE PEEL, TO TASTE (OPTIONAL)

Butter a 9" × 13" baking pan and sprinkle with some breadcrumbs. Tap the side of the pan to remove excess crumbs.
Mix flour and baking powder together on a large work surface. Add butter and cut in with a knife, very fine. Add powdered sugar and mix well. Make a well in the mixture. Add yolks, one by one, and stir into dough. With addition of each egg, more dough becomes moistened. Finish mixing, using the hands. Make a well in the

dough. Add oil and sour cream. Working from the center out, blend ingredients together. Dough will be soft. Divide in half, and add cocoa to one half. Work cocoa into the dough with a spoon. Freeze the dough containing cocoa until it is hard; it will be grated later. Refrigerate the other half of the dough until it is hard enough to roll. It should be ready by the time the middle layer is made.

To make the middle layer, grind cheese twice in a food grinder or mix in a processor until it is smooth and pastelike. Do not mix too long in processor or the cheese will become watery. In a bowl, blend ground cheese, sugar, baking powder and sour cream. Beat egg whites until frothy. Add sugar and continue beating until the whites are stiff but not dry. Gently fold into cheese mixture. Add both types of flour and blend well. If desired, add raisins or candied orange peel to taste. Set aside.

To make the bottom layer, remove the chilled dough (contains no cocoa) from the refrigerator and roll out on a lightly floured board to the dimensions of the pan. To get the dough in the pan, roll it around the rolling pin and then unroll it into the pan. The dough is quite soft, so it can be manipulated easily if the rolled slab is larger or smaller than the pan. Put cheese mixture on top of the dough in the pan.

To make the top layer, remove dough containing cocoa from the freezer and grate it over the cheese layer, covering it uniformly. Put pan into oven preheated to 350°F. After 5 minutes increase temperature to 375°F. In another 5 minutes, increase temperature to 400°F. Continue baking cake for another 40–50 minutes at 400°F. Cool in pan until just slightly warm, then turn upside down to remove. If served upside down, top with a chocolate sauce.

### Ciasto Makowe z Musem Serowym

*"Duet," a layered poppy seed and white cheese mousse.* Serves 6.

This recipe was provided by Bernard Lussiana, executive head chef of Warsaw's Hotel Le Royal Meridien Bristol. Chef Lussiana uses a traditional Polish ingredient, the poppy seed, to create this elegant dessert.

*Poppy seed base*

1⅓ CUP POPPY SEEDS

1¼ CUPS WHOLE MILK

1 LARGE EGG

1 OUNCE BUTTER

3 TABLESPOONS HONEY

4 TEASPOONS SUGAR

¼ CUP RAISINS

1 DROP VANILLA EXTRACT

[Ciasto Makowe z Musem Serowym, *continued*]

    1 DROP ALMOND EXTRACT

    PARCHMENT PAPER

    *White cheese mousse*

    3 EGG YOLKS

    3 OUNCES NATURAL YOGURT

    3 OUNCES WHITE CREAM CHEESE

    8 OUNCES WHIPPED CREAM (36% FAT)

    4 TABLESPOONS SUGAR

    2 TABLESPOONS WATER

    2 TEASPOONS KNOX UNFLAVORED GELATIN POWDER

    1 TABLESPOON HOT WATER

    *Vodka syrup*

    5 OUNCES SUGAR

    1¼ CUP MINERAL WATER

    ⅔ CUP PREMIUM CYTRYNÓWKA VODKA*

    2½ TEASPOONS KNOX UNFLAVORED GELATIN POWDER

    1 DROP YELLOW FOOD COLORING

    *Garnish*

    FRESH MINT

    FRESH FLOWERS

Place rectangular, bottomless pan (4½" × 14" × 1")† on sheet of parchment paper on cookie tray.

Simmer poppy seeds and milk in saucepan until all liquid is absorbed, stirring continuously at the end. Cool mixture and grind twice in mechanical grinder or in large mortar and pestle. Put ground poppy seeds in a bowl and add remaining ingredients for poppy seed base, mixing well. Fill pan with mixture and bake 20 minutes in oven preheated to 350°F. Let cooked mixture cool in pan.

Whisk egg yolks in heat-resistant bowl and set aside. Mix together yogurt and cream cheese until smooth, and set aside. Whip cream and set aside. Cook sugar with water until temperature reaches 250°F and slowly pour it on yolks, whisking rapidly during addition. Avoid pouring the sugar mixture directly on the whisk, as it will harden there. Mix gelatin with hot water and quickly add to egg and sugar mixture, stirring well. Continue to whisk until mixture reaches room temperature. Blend in cheese and yogurt mixture. Gently fold in whipped cream. Put mixture on top of cooled poppy seed layer and refrigerate for 4 hours.

To make the vodka syrup, boil sugar with water. Add gelatin and mix until melted.

Turn off heat and stir in vodka and food coloring. Refrigerate for at least 4 hours. Cut the "duet" into three four-inch squares, and cut each square diagonally into two triangles. Then cut each triangle into three different-sized triangles. Arrange the three triangles like a fan on a chilled plate. Decorate with mint and fresh flowers (be sure to select a nontoxic variety such as fresia or violets). Pour a small amount of sauce around the triangles and serve immediately.

*Cytrynówka is a lemon-flavored Polish vodka available at specialty liquor stores. If not available, add some lemon zest to boiling water with sugar to taste and steep at room temperature for 24 hours. Strain and add to unflavored vodka to taste.

†This pan is called a flan frame. See *Resources* (p. 65) for mail-order suppliers. The sides of a tart pan (without the removable bottom) with similar dimensions can be substituted. The edges of these tart pans are usually fluted, but this will not matter because the edges of the dessert will be trimmed.

## Mazurek Orzechowy

*Walnut mazurka, a flat cake with ground walnuts.* Serves many.

This recipe was provided by Ewa Bartkowiak. She is a native of Poznań, the major city of the region of Poland called Wielkopolska (Great Poland).

$^3$/$_{16}$-INCH WAFER SHEET FOR CRUST (*WAFLE TORTOWE*)*

   *Filling*

½ CUP BUTTER

1¼ CUP SUGAR

3 EGG YOLKS

8 OUNCES WALNUT MEATS, FINELY GROUND

¾ CUP FLOUR

   *Meringue topping*

3 EGG WHITES

½ CUP SUGAR

Cut wafer to fit bottom of pan, piecing if necessary. The walnut mixture will hold the pieces together nicely.

Cream butter and sugar together, then stir in egg yolks and blend well. Add walnuts and flour to mixture at same time and stir until well mixed. Spread mixture evenly on top of wafer.

Beat egg whites with electric beater until foamy. Slowly add sugar and continue beating until stiff peaks form. Spread evenly on top of walnut mixture. Bake for about 1 hour at 300°F. The meringue should be golden brown.

*Available in markets carrying Polish foods; also see *Resources* (p. 65) for mail-order suppliers.

## Miscellaneous

### Proziaki

*Peasant bread.* Serves many.

Teresa Palka, who is originally from the village of Grodzisko in southeastern Poland, provided this recipe. She now resides in Rzeszów, the major city of this region in the Carpathian foothills.

1.1 POUNDS FLOUR (ABOUT 4⅓ CUPS)

½ TEASPOON SODA

½ TEASPOON SALT

1 EGG

1½ CUPS BUTTERMILK

VEGETABLE OIL FOR FRYING

Sift flour, soda and salt onto a large work surface. Make a well in the center of the mixture and put egg and 1 cup buttermilk in well. With a knife, begin blending the flour mixture with the liquid in the well, beginning at the inside edge of the flour mixture. Add the rest of buttermilk to the well and continue mixing with the knife until the flour mixture is well blended with the liquid ingredients. The dough should be slightly sticky. On a floured board, roll dough out to ¼-inch thickness and cut into 1½" × 2" pieces. Put oil into a frying pan to a depth of about ½ inch and heat on medium setting. Add several pieces of dough and reduce heat. Fry until light brown on both sides. If the oil is too hot, the dough will darken too quickly and be incompletely cooked inside. Cool on paper towels. Peasant bread is especially good while still warm.

### Kiełbasa

*Polish sausage.* Serves many.

David Peterson, co-author of *Eat Smart in Poland,* provided this recipe. He is the owner of the Regent Sausage Company in Madison, Wisconsin.

2½ POUNDS LEAN PORK

½ POUND PORK FAT

*or*

3 POUNDS PORK SHOULDER/BUTT

1½ TABLESPOONS SALT

1 TABLESPOON BLACK PEPPER, COARSELY GROUND

2 TABLESPOONS FRESH GARLIC, MINCED

1 TABLESPOON MARJORAM

1 TABLESPOON GROUND CORIANDER

1 TABLESPOON DRY MUSTARD

1 SMALL ONION, FINELY CHOPPED OR 2 TABLESPOONS ONION POWDER

¼ TABLESPOON POWDERED BAY LEAF

¼ TABLESPOON ALLSPICE

½ CUP ICE WATER

Grind meat coarsely (using a ⅜-inch or a ½-inch plate). Mix well with remaining ingredients. Stuff into 32–35 mm hog casings. Twist into 6–8 inch links (or desired length). Dry 24 hours in refrigerator, turning once. The sausages can be frozen or kept for a few days in the refrigerator before cooking. They can be grilled, pan fried, boiled, broiled or baked. If used in other dishes, they should be gently simmered for 15 minutes, cooled and sliced as needed.

### Ogórki Kiszone

*Pickled cucumbers.* Serves many.

This recipe was provided by Marcin Filutowicz, Professor of Bacteriology at the University of Wisconsin in Madison. It was adapted from a recipe created by his family (grandfather Prof. Stanislaw Rosnowski and father Prof. Antoni Filutowicz), who lived in Bydgoszcz in the northwestern part of Poland called Pomerania.

*Per quart pickles*

8–10 FRESHLY PICKED CUCUMBERS, WASHED

2 FRESH GRAPE LEAVES, WASHED

3 FRESH SOUR CHERRY LEAVES, WASHED

1 TABLESPOON MUSTARD SEEDS

2 CLOVES GARLIC

1 STEM DILL WITH SEEDS

HORSERADISH LEAF, 2" × 2" PIECE WITH STEM OR GENEROUS SHAVING OF
    HORSERADISH ROOT

1 QUART KERR OR BALL STANDARD CANNING JAR*

1 QUART WATER BOTTLED IN PLASTIC

2 TABLESPOONS KOSHER SALT (MORTON BRAND)

Put 1 grape leaf, cherry leaves, mustard seeds, 1 garlic clove, dill and horseradish leaf into canning jar. Tightly pack cucumbers on top, positioning the last one almost horizontally to help keep all cucumbers below the pickling brine. Top with another grape leaf and garlic clove.

[Ogórki Kiszone, *continued*]

Dissolve salt in water and fill jar to within ¼ inch from the top. In order to get crispy pickles that keep well for a year, it is critical to use bottled water and Morton brand kosher salt. Cap the jars loosely and keep in a cool place (55–60°F). Fermentation typically takes five to six weeks. Quick-eating pickles (ready in 2–3 weeks) can be made by lowering the salt concentration to 1½ tablespoons of salt per quart of water and allowing fermentation to occur at room temperature. Fermentation depends on *Lactobacillus species,* which produces a mild acid (lactic acid). Lactobacilli are soil bacteria that inhabit all vegetables in contact with soil. (Sauerkraut production depends on the same bacteria.) Fermentation must be slow in jars that are not closed too tightly. As fermentation proceeds, the rapidly evolving carbon dioxide must be able to escape. Some oozing of brine is almost unavoidable. Bubbling at the surface will not be detectable. After fermentation is complete, tighten the lids. If lids are tightened too early, the trapped carbon dioxide will macerate the tissue and the pickles will get soft after three to five months. If lids are not tightened at the end, various fungi could get in and cause spoilage.

Note: salt and lactic acid are the only preservatives in these pickles.

*Choose jars that withstand high temperatures and pressure.

# Shopping in Poland's Food Markets

## Helpful Tips

### The Open-Air Markets

Learning more about Polish food in an outdoor market setting is a lot of fun. These markets usually are centrally located. Since some are not open every day of the week, be sure to get a schedule of the days they are open so you won't be disappointed. The greatest activity often occurs early in the morning. Non-food items also will be available.

Food in the markets is sold by the kilogram (kilo, or kg). To encourage sales, vendors often offer generous samples to taste. This is a good opportunity to ask for the name of an item that is not labeled. If you would like to give Polish a try, see *Helpful Phrases* (p. 69). The vendors, and many of the other Poles around you, will be happy to answer questions.

Some items to look for in the outdoor markets are dried wild mushrooms, especially the *borowik,* or king bolete mushroom. Long strings of them hang in the stalls. The small wild or alpine strawberry (*poziomka*) is a delicate taste treat, as is the wild blueberry (*czernica*). There will be several varieties of homemade farmer's cheese and other milk products, such as *kefir,* a yogurt-like beverage. In Zakopane, in the Tatra Mountain area, smoked sheep's milk cheese is sold near the funicular to Mt. Gubałówka. Ladies sit all day behind their small tables piled high with cheeses molded with various shapes and surface designs. On the outskirts of Poznań is an enormous wholesale food market well worth a visit. Huge displays of every imaginable food product can be found outdoors as well as inside several long buildings lined up in a row. This market, Franowo, comes alive around 2 AM, and remains open until early afternoon.

## A Health Precaution

Wherever you travel, choose your food vendors with care, following the same criteria used at home. Don't ask for trouble. Some serious diseases can be transmitted by eating unclean produce. Make sure the produce looks fresh and clean. Should there be any doubt, look for stalls that appear popular with the local people.

## The Supermarkets

Be sure to shop in the large, modern supermarkets (*supersam or sam spożywczy*) as well. Also visit the immense and awesome market hall called Hala Targowa in Wrocław. These markets are a wonderful place to get the makings for a tasty picnic featuring Polish food. For convenience, remember to pack some lightweight tableware and a pocket knife before leaving home!

The following abbreviated list of weights in Polish proved sufficient to get the quantities we desired. Corresponding approximate weights in pounds are included.

> 25 decagrams: *dwadzieścia pięć dkg* (*dekagram*)
> = *ćwierć kilo:* quarter kilo, or ½ pound

> 50 decagrams: *pięćdziesiąt dkg* (*dekagram*)
> = *pół kilo:* half kilo, or 1 pound

If you are considering bringing food back to the United States, check with the US Customs Service beforehand to see which items or categories of items are allowed. Ask for the latest edition of publication number 512. Changes in regulations that occurred after publication can be obtained by writing to:

Assistant Commissioner
Office of Inspection and Control
US Customs Service
Washington, DC 20229

# Resources

## Mail-Order Suppliers of Polish Food Items

Polish ingredients can be found in stores specializing in Polish foods and in many supermarkets. There are close to 10 million Polish Americans and Polish delis are scattered around the country to serve them. One can find a wide array of foods from the "old country," including sausages, cold cuts, *pierogi,* cheeses and other milk products, honey cakes, dried wild mushrooms, canned goods and specialty vodkas.

Some mail-order suppliers of Polish food items are listed below. Most have a catalog or brochure of their products, and some have websites. We would appreciate knowing if a listed store no longer handles mail orders. Please also bring to our attention mail-order suppliers of Polish ingredients not included here. If you prefer to shop in a store, we can provide assistance in locating a Polish deli near you.

At the end of each store's listing, we named the item(s) carried that are needed for recipes in this guidebook. If mail-ordering Polish (or European-style) farmer's cheese, specify cheese made with whole milk. Note that cheese is costly to ship. It can be made with little effort at home, however, and we welcome inquiries from those interested in learning how to make their own farmer's cheese.

Redlinski Meats
2333 Bowen Rd.
Elma, NY 14059
Tel: 800-867-4060
Fax: 716-655-6407
http://www.redlinski.com
(cheese; dried wild mushrooms)

Polish Art Center
9539 Joseph Campau Ave.
Hamtramck, MI 48212
Tel: 888-619-9771
Fax: 313-874-1302
www.polartcenter.com
(dried wild mushrooms)

Bridge Kitchenware
214 E. 52nd St.
New York, NY 10022
Tel: 800-274-3435
Tel: 212-838-1901
Fax: 212-758-5387
www.bridgekitchenware.com
Item #: ABTF-PR-14
(flan frame for walnut *mazurka*)

Pol-Store
PO Box 140914
Staten Island, NY 10314
Tel: 888-POL-STORE
Fax: 718-720-5810
www.polstore.com
(dried wild mushrooms)

R. Hirt, Jr. Co.
2468 Market St.
Detroit, MI 48207-4597
Tel: 313-567-1173
Fax: 313-567-8123
(Old-European style farmer's cheese )

G.Q.F. Mfg Co.
PO Box 1552
Savannah, GA 31402-1552
Tel: 912-236-0651
Fax: 912-234-9978
(quail eggs)

We can provide wafer sheets (*wafle tortowe*), beet sour (*barszcz czerwony*) and vegetable base. Please contact us for details.

Ginkgo Press, Inc.
Tel: 608-233-5488
Fax: 608-233-0053
ginkgo@ginkgopress.com

# *Travel Agencies*

The following travel agencies offer a wide variety of special tours. Both have a tour to interest food lovers traveling to Poland. Air ToursPoland offers the "Connoisseur Tour: Great Art and Cuisine of Poland." Craft World Tours offers "Folk Crafts from the Baltic Coast to the High Tatras." The folk craft tour includes visits to many of Poland's small, open-air museums (*skansen*), each of which is a cluster of preserved homesteads and farm buildings with interesting ethnographic collections, including old household equipment. One can learn about regional peasant cookery and sample some dishes to get the pulse of the region. These tours operate on demand, so please inquire about their status during your anticipated travel time.

Air Tours Poland
LOT Airlines
500 Fifth Ave., Suite 408
New York, NY 10110
Tel: 212-852-0243
Fax: 212-302-0191
e-mail: airtours@lot.com

Sherry Wilson
Craft World Tours
6776 Warboys Rd.
Byron, NY 14422
Tel: 716-548-2667

# Some Useful Organizations to Know About

## Polish National Tourism Offices

The address listed below is for the Polish Tourism Office. The staff can assist you with your travel planning. We suggest that you visit the website (www.polandtour.org) of the tourism office to request travel materials.

275 Madison Ave., Suite 1711
New York, NY 10016
Tel: 212-338-9412
Fax: 212-338-9283

## International Organizations

We are members of two international organizations that exist to promote good will and understanding between people of different cultures. These organizations, Servas and The Friendship Force, share similar ideals but operate somewhat differently.

### Servas

Servas, from the Esperanto word meaning "serve," is a non-profit system of travelers and hosts. Servas members travel independently and make their own contacts with fellow members in other countries, choosing hosts with attributes of interest from membership rosters. It is a wonderful way to get to know people, be invited into their homes as a family member, share experiences and help promote world peace.

For more information about membership in Servas, write or call:

US Servas Committee, Inc.
11 John St., Suite #407
New York, NY 10038
Tel: 212-267-0252

## *The Friendship Force*

The Friendship Force is a non-profit organization, which also fosters good will through encounters between people of different backgrounds. Unlike Servas, Friendship Force members travel in groups to host countries. Both itinerary and travel arrangements are made by a member acting as exchange director. These trips combine stays with a host family and group travel within the host country.

For more information on membership in The Friendship Force, write:

The Friendship Force
One CNN Center
Suite 575, South Tower
Atlanta, GA 30303

# Helpful Phrases

## For Use in Restaurants and Food Markets

### In the Restaurant

The following list of phrases in Polish will assist you in ordering food, learning more about the dish you ordered, and determining what specialties of a region are available. Each phrase also is written phonetically to help with pronunciation. Note that the sound of the letter "g" is as in "get." Syllables in capital letters are accented and underlined letters are essentially silent. You will discover that Poles heartily encourage your attempt to converse with them in Polish. By all means, give it a try at every opportunity.

| | |
|---|---|
| DO YOU HAVE A MENU? | Czy macie jadłospis? |
| | *Chih* MAH-*chyeh yahd*-WAHS-*pees?* |
| MAY I SEE THE MENU? | Czy mogę zobaczyć jadłospis? |
| | *Chih* MOH-*geh zoh*-BAH-*cheetsh yahd-*WAHS-*pees?* |
| WHAT DO YOU RECOMMEND? | Co pan (male)/pani (female) poleca? |
| | *Tsoh pahn/*PAHN-*ee poh*-LEHTS-*ah?* |
| DO YOU HAVE . . . ? (ADD AN ITEM FROM THE *MENU GUIDE* OR THE *FOODS & FLAVORS GUIDE*.) | Czy macie . . . ? |
| | *Chih* MAH-*chyeh* . . . ? |

# Helpful Phrases

WHAT IS THE "SPECIAL" FOR TODAY?

Co jest specjalnego dzisiaj?
*Tsoh yehst speh-tsyahl-NEH-GOH JEE-shy?*

DO YOU HAVE ANY SPECIAL REGIONAL DISH?

Czy macie specjalną potrawę charakterystyczną dla tej okolicy?
*Chih MAH-chyeh speh-TSYAHL-nawn poh-TRAH-veh hah-rahk-teh-rees-TEECH-nawn dlah teh oh-koh-LITS-ee?*

IS THIS DISH SPICY?

Czy ta potrawa jest pikantna?
*Chih tah poh-TRAH-vah yehst pee-KAHNT-nah?*

WE WOULD LIKE TO ORDER . . .

My chcemy zamówić . . .
*Meh hit-SEH-meh zah-MOO-veetsh . . .*

WHAT ARE THE INGREDIENTS IN THIS DISH?

Jakie są składniki tej potrawy?
*YAH-kyeh sawn skwad-NEEK-ee teh poh-TRAH-veh?*

WHAT ARE THE SEASONINGS IN THIS DISH?

Jakie przyprawy są w tej potrawie?
*YAH-kyeh pshee-PRAH-veh sawn vuh teh poh-TRAH-vee-eh?*

THANK YOU VERY MUCH. THE FOOD IS DELICIOUS.

Dziękuję bardzo, ta potrawa jest smaczna.
*Jehn-KOO-yeh BAHR-dzoh, tah poh-TRAH-vah yehst SMAHCH-nah.*

## In the Market

The following phrases will help you make purchases and learn more about unfamiliar produce, spices and herbs.

WHAT ARE THE REGIONAL
FRUITS AND VEGETABLES?

Jakie są owoce i jarzyny charakterystyczne dla tej okolicy (tego rejonu)?

*YAH-kyeh sawn oh-VOH-tseh ee yah-ZHEE-neh hah-rahk-teh-rees-TEECH-neh dla teh oh-koh-LITS-ee (TEH-goh reh-OH-new)?*

WHAT IS THIS CALLED?

Jak się to nazywa?

*Yahk shyeh toh nah-ZEE-vah?*

DO YOU HAVE . . . ?
(ADD AN ITEM FROM THE
FOODS & FLAVORS GUIDE.)

Czy macie . . . ?

*Chih MAH-chyeh . . . ?*

MAY I TASTE THIS?

Czy mogę spróbować?

*Chih MOH-geh sprooh-BOH-vach?*

WHERE CAN I BUY
FRESH . . . ?

Gdzie mogę kupić świeże . . . ?

*Gehjeh MOH-geh KOO-peetsh SHVYEH-zheh . . . ?*

HOW MUCH IS THIS PER
KILOGRAM (KG)?

Ile kosztuje kilogram (kg)?

*EE-leh kosh-TOO-yeh kee-LOH-grahm (kg)?*

I WOULD LIKE TO BUY ½ KILO-
GRAM (KG) OF THIS/THAT.

Chcę kupić pół kilograma (kg) tego/tamtego.

*Htseh KOO-peetsh poow kee-loh-GRAH-mah (kg) TEH-goh/tahm-TEH-goh.*

MAY I PHOTOGRAPH THIS?

Czy mogę zrobić zdjęcie (foto) tego?

*Chih MOH-geh ZROH-beech ZDYEHN-cheh FOH-toh TEH-goh?*

**OTHER**

## Other Useful Phrases

Sometimes it helps to see in writing a word or phrase that is said to you in Polish, because certain letters have distinctly different sounds in Polish than in English. You may be familiar with the word and its English translation but less familiar with its pronunciation. The following phrase comes in handy if you want to see the word or phrase you are hearing.

PLEASE WRITE IT ON MY PIECE OF PAPER.

Proszę napisać na moim papierze.

*PROH-sheh  nah-PEE-sach  nah  MOH-eem  pah-pee-EHR-zjeh.*

Interested in bringing home books about Polish food?

WHERE CAN I BUY A POLISH COOKBOOK IN ENGLISH?

Gdzie mogę kupić polską książkę kucharską po angielsku?

*Gehjeh  MOH-geh  KOO-peetsh  POHL-skawn  KSHONZH-keh  koo-HAHR-skawn  poh  ahn-GYEHL-skoo?*

And, of course, the following phrases also are useful to know.

WHERE IS THE MEN'S /LADIES' RESTROOM?

Gdzie jest toaleta męska/damska?

*Gehjeh  yehst  toh-ah-LEH-tah  MEH-skah/DAHM-skah?*

MAY I HAVE THE CHECK, PLEASE?

Poproszę o rachunek?

*Poh-PROH-sheh  oh  rah-HOO-nehk?*

DO YOU ACCEPT CREDIT CARDS? TRAVELERS CHECKS?

Czy przyjmujecie karty kredytowe? Travel czeki?

*Chih  pshee-moo-YEH-tsheh  KAHR-tee  kreh-dee-TOH-veh?  TRAH-vehl  CHECK-ee?*

# Menu Guide

This alphabetical listing is an extensive compilation of menu entries in Polish, with English translations, to make ordering food easy. It includes typical Polish dishes as well as specialties characteristic of the different regions of the country.

Classic regional dishes of Poland that should not be missed are labeled "regional classic" in the margin next to the menu entry. Outside a particular geographical area, however, these specialties may not be available unless a restaurant features one or more regional cuisines. Some noteworthy dishes popular throughout much of the country—also not to be missed—are labeled "national favorite." Comments on some of our favorites also are included in the margin.

With *Eat Smart in Poland* in hand, you will quickly become more familiar with restaurant cuisine. Be sure to take it with you when you shop in the markets or dine. Breakfast (*śniadanie*) at home consists of bread, butter, jam, cold cuts and farmer's cheese, along with coffee or tea, and it typically is eaten between 5 and 8 AM because work begins early in the day. A second, lighter breakfast (*drugie śniadanie*), usually a sandwich and coffee or milk, is taken later in the morning at work. The day's main meal (*obiad*) is eaten after work between 3 and 6 PM. It is a substantial meal typically beginning with a hearty soup followed by a meat or fish entrée, along with vegetables and probably potatoes, which are especially enjoyed boiled. Soup could also be followed with a pasta dish such as *pierogi,* the well-known semicircular pillows containing meat, sauerkraut or potato and cheese fillings. The main dish also is accompanied by a dinner salad. Dessert is often cake served with coffee or tea. The last meal of the day—*kolacja* (meaning cold cuts)—is a light, cold supper, similar in content to breakfast, which usually is taken between 7 and 8 PM.

Restaurants serving breakfast open around 9 AM; otherwise, they open about noon. In small towns, it may not be possible to dine out after 8 PM. Metropolitan areas, however, will have food available until late in the evening. Hot and cold evening meals are served at restaurants.

**ajerkoniak** eggnog vodka.

**auszpik z kaczek** duck in aspic.

**awanturka** spread of cottage cheese and sardines.

**baba wielkanocna** Easter version of the holiday and special-occasion sweet yeast cake called *baba* or *babka* (see *Foods & Flavors Guide*). Citron, candied orange and lemon peel, raisins and almonds are added to the dough, and the cake is decorated with icing and colored sugar or baker's confetti.

**babeczka migałowa** cupcake with almonds.

**babeczka z morelami** cupcake with apricots.

**babka podolska** Podolian-style *babka* with plums. Podole was a part of southeastern Poland that was incorporated into the Soviet Union after World War II. It is a notable plum-growing area.

**babki śmietankowe** *babka* filled with custard.

**babki z wątróbek** savory cake with minced liver, onions, breadcrumbs and egg yolks.

**bakłażany faszerowane mięsem** eggplant stuffed with meat.

**banan opiekany** toasted banana.

**baranina duszona z fasolą** lamb stewed with beans.

**baranina duszona z włoską kapustą** braised lamb with savoy cabbage.

**barszcz botwinkowy** seasonal variation of beet soup made with grated young beets and finely cut young beet leaves, sour cream and pieces of hard-boiled egg. Also called *boćwinka* and *botwina*.

**barszcz czerwony z kulebiakiem** beet soup served with a pastry roll typically filled with meat or mushrooms. The pastry usually is made in a long roll and sliced into individual servings.

**barszcz czerwony z paluszkami** beet soup served with stick crackers.

**barszcz czerwony z pasztecikem** beet soup served with a small, savory pastry.

**barszcz postny** meatless beet soup made with vegetable stock rather than meat stock. It is a typical Lenten dish.

**barszcz ukraiński** Ukrainian beet soup with sour cream and vegetables. Typical additions to beets are potatoes, savoy cabbage, tomatoes and navy beans. (Ukraine, or Red Ruthenia, was once a part of the Lithuanian/Polish Empire.)

**barszcz z kołdunami** beet soup with small lamb- or mushroom-filled round or half-round pastas.

**barszcz z uszkami** clear beet soup with tiny pasta squares that have been folded over a mushroom filling to form a triangle and pinched together at two ends. It is traditionally eaten at the Christmas Eve supper (*wigilia*) and therefore is also named *barszcz czysty wigilijny*. See recipe, p. 43.   NATIONAL FAVORITE

**barszcz zabielany** beet soup with sour cream.

**bażant pieczony** roasted pheasant.

**befsztyk tatarski** steak tartare; also called *befsztyk po tatarsku*.

**befsztyk z polędwicy** beef tenderloin steak.

**befsztyk z polędwicy w sosie lwowskim** beef tenderloin with a sauce in the style of the formerly Polish city of Lwów.   REGIONAL CLASSIC

**befsztyki z cebulą** steak with onions.

**biała kiełbasa** fresh (not smoked) pork sausage with garlic.

**biała kiełbasa duszona w piwie** fresh (not smoked) pork sausage stewed in beer.

**biała kiełbasa w sosie pomidorowym** fresh (not smoked) pork sausage in tomato sauce.

**biała kiełbasa z kapustą** fresh (not smoked) pork sausage and sauerkraut.   NATIONAL FAVORITE

**białucha** white soup made with sour milk and smoked bacon.

**biały barszcz** tart soup made of fermented rye bread with slices of sausage (*kiełbasa*) and hard-boiled egg. It is a traditional Easter dish in areas of eastern Poland. Elsewhere the soup is called *żurek*.   REGIONAL CLASSIC

**bigos** hunter's stew, a classic dish containing cabbage, sauerkraut and a variety of meats, game and smoked sausage. See recipe, p. 40.   NATIONAL FAVORITE

**bigos z indykiem** hunter's stew with turkey.

**bigos z soplicowa** stew of cabbage and shredded pork.

**bita śmietana z rodzynkami** whipped cream with raisins.

**bite kotlety** pounded cutlets.

**bite zrazy** pounded fillets; the name of this dish is frequently shortened to *bitki*.

**bitki cielęce w śmietanie** pounded veal scallops cooked in sour cream.

**bitki śledziowe** pounded herring fillets.   GOOD CHOICE

**bitki we sosie własnym** pounded beef steak in its own juices.

**bitki z pulardy** pounded chicken breast.

**boczek duszony z kapustą** stewed bacon and cabbage.

**boczek pieczony** roasted bacon.

**boczek wędzony wypiekany** baked smoked bacon.

NATIONAL FAVORITE **botwina** a seasonal variation of beet soup made with grated young beets and finely cut young beet leaves, cream and pieces of hard-boiled egg. Other names for *botwina* are *boćwinka* and *barszcz botwinkowy*.

**brukiew duszona z kartoflami** stewed rutabagas and potatoes.

**brukselka po polsku** Polish-style Brussels sprouts topped with breadcrumbs sautéed in butter.

REGIONAL CLASSIC **bryndzowe hałuski** dumplings made from sheep's cheese (*bryndza*) and grated raw potatoes. It is a traditional dish of the Tatra Mountain region of southern Poland.

**brzoskwinie w araku** peaches in rum.

**buchty** small, fruit-filled buns.

**budyń cielęcy** calf's brain pudding.

**budyń z chleba** bread pudding.

**budyń z duszonej wątróbki** liver pudding.

**budyń z maku** poppy seed pudding.

**budyń z ryżu** rice pudding.

**budyń z szynki** ham pudding.

NATIONAL FAVORITE **bukiet z jarzyn** mixture of shredded raw and pickled vegetables; also called *bukiet z warzyw* and *bukiet surówek*.

**bułeczka** small wheat bun.

**bułka paryska** baguette.

**bułka z pieczarkami** baguette stuffed with mushrooms, a fast-food item sold from food carts on the streets.

TASTY **buraczki z jabłkami** braised beets with apples.

**cebulak** onion rolls.

**cebulka glazowana** glazed shallots.

**chleb ze smalcem i ogórkiem** bread served with cucumbers and a spread of fat studded with onion and cracklings.

NATIONAL FAVORITE **chłodnik** cold, summertime soup with young beets and beet greens, sour milk and beet juice, and various other ingredients such as chopped cucumbers, onions, radishes and parsley, typically served over sliced or quartered hard-boiled eggs; also called *chłodnik litewski* (Lithuanian *chłodnik*). See color insert, p. 7.

**chłodnik jabłkowy** cold apple soup.

**chłodnik z truskawek i agrestu** cold strawberry and gooseberry soup.

**chrupki** savory, crisp biscuits or cookies.

**chruściki** traditional pre-Lenten "angel wing" cookies made by taking small, thin rectangles of dough, cutting a slit in the middle and pulling one end through the slit. They are then fried and dusted with powdered sugar. Other names for these cookies are *chrust* and *faworki*.

**ciasteczka polskie z galeretką** Polish cookies made with pastry dough containing sieved eggs. Unbaked cookies have a central depression made with the finger, which is filled with warmed jelly after the baked cookies have cooled.

**ciasto makowe z musem serowym** layered poppy seed and white cheese mousse. See recipe, p. 57.

**cielęcina w majonezie** veal with mayonnaise.

**cielęcina w złotych płatkach** breaded and fried veal roll with cheese.

**cielęcina z nerką** veal with kidney.

**cielęcina z papryką** veal with paprika.

**cocktail truskawkowy** strawberry milk shake.

**cocktail z czarnej porzeczki** black currant milk shake.

**comber cielęcy** roasted rack of veal.

**comber cielęcy a la duchesse** rack of veal in sour cream sauce, garnished with crayfish and sliced truffles.

**comber jeleni ze śmietaną** saddle of venison basted with sour cream.

**comber sarni** saddle of venison.

**comber z sarny w naturalnym sosie z kluseczkami** saddle of venison au jus with dumplings.

**cynaderki cielęce smażone** fried veal kidneys.

**cynaderki z grzybami** kidneys with mushrooms.

**cynadry wołowe z pieczarkami** beef kidney with mushrooms.

**czarna polewka** black soup; this version of duck blood soup historically was served to a rejected suitor by a girl's family to signify that his marrying her was out of the question.

**czernina** creamy, sweet-sour duck blood soup with raisins and prunes, flavored with allspice and cloves; also spelled *czarnina*. Another name for this soup is *jusznik*. Also see *czarna polewka*.

**czernina na żeberkach** duck blood soup with pork ribs.

**NATIONAL FAVORITE**    **ćwikła z chrzanem** relish of pickled beets with horseradish. It is traditionally served on holidays, especially Christmas and Easter. Also simply called *ćwikła*.

**dorsz w sosie chrzanowym** cod with horseradish sauce.

**duszona wołowina z grzybami** stewed beef with mushrooms.

**dynia duszona w śmietanie** stewed pumpkin with sour cream.

**dziad** gnarly, many-layered cake resembling a tree trunk, which is baked on a horizonal, rotating spit over a fire. Over 50 eggs and two pounds of butter, flour and sugar each are needed to make it. The first layer is made by pouring a ladleful of the liquid batter onto the hot spit. When this layer is baked, another layer of batter is poured and allowed to bake. Successive layers are added and baked until the batter is gone. Uneven baking creates the surface gnarls which resemble those on the cane of a beggar (*dziad*) for which it is named. When cooked, the cake is removed from the spit, set in a vertical position and cross-wise slices are cut, displaying the annual growth rings of the "tree." Another name for this cake is *sękacz*. It is thought to have originated from Germany where it is known as *baumkuchen*. Today it is made primarily in the Suwałki region in the far northeastern corner of Poland.

**dzika kaczka w czerwonej kapuście** wild duck in red cabbage.

**dziki gołąb w sosie porzeczkowym** wild pigeon in currant sauce.

**dziki królik smażony** fried wild rabbit.

**GREAT**    **dzikie kaczki pieczone** roasted wild duck.

**fasola po francusku** French-style green beans.

**fasola sucha z masłem** dried beans with butter.

**fasolka po bretońsku** Brittany-style beans: beans, bacon and sausage in tomato-based sauce flavored with paprika.

**REGIONAL CLASSIC**    **fasolka szparagowa po poznańsku** Poznań-style wax beans simmered in milk thickened with flour.

**fasolka z masłem** green beans with butter.

**NATIONAL FAVORITE**    **faworki** traditional pre-Lenten "angel wing" cookies. (See *chrust*, this *Guide*).

**filet z kurczaka w cieście piwnym** chicken breast encased in beer-containing dough.

**filet z soli z tartym serem** fillet of sole with grated cheese.

**flaczki po lwowsku** Lwów-style broth-based tripe soup with carrots and meat, flavored with caraway. The city of Lwów was in the part of eastern Poland that was incorporated into the Soviet Union after World War II. It is now called L'viv.

**flaczki po warszawsku** Warsaw-style tripe and vegetables in cream sauce, seasoned with nutmeg, marjoram and ginger.    REGIONAL CLASSIC

**forszmak** creamy, tomato-based goulash with meat and sausage.

**frykadelki cielęce** veal sausage rolls.

**frytki** French fries.

**galaretka truskawkowa** small, molded gelatin dessert with strawberries.

**galarekta z nóżek wieprzowych** jellied pig's knuckles or trotters; also called *studzienina* and *zimne nogi*.

**galaretka z owoców** small, molded gelatin dessert with fruit.

**gęsia szyjka faszerowana** deboned goose neck skin stuffed with a mixture of ground veal and mushrooms and boiled.    DELICIOUS

**gęś duszona w czarnym sosie** goose braised in black sauce, a sweet-sour blend of goose blood, honey, cloves, ginger, allspice and vinegar.

**gęś nadziewana fasolą** roasted goose with bean stuffing.

**gęś pieczona** roasted goose.

**gęś pieczona nadziewana kasztanami** roasted goose with chestnut stuffing.

**gęś po kaszubsku** Kashubian-style goose cooked in pickle juice    REGIONAL CLASSIC with potatoes and rutabagas, flavored with dill and allspice. Kashubia encompasses an area of about 70 miles southwest of the city of Gdańsk, in the region of Pomerania.

**gęś w miodzie z czerwoną kapustą** goose in honey with red cabbage.

**gicz cielęca** leg of veal steamed on the bone.

**główka cielęca w sosie pomidorowym** calf's head in tomato sauce.

**golonka gotowana** boiled pork shanks; also called *golonka*    NATIONAL FAVORITE *wieprzowa*. See color insert, p. 1.

**golonka z rusztu** grilled pork shanks; also called *golonka z grilla*.

**gołąb pieczony** baked pigeon.

**gołąbki** hot stuffed cabbage rolls.    NATIONAL FAVORITE

**REGIONAL CLASSIC** **gołąbki po kurpiowsku** Kurpie-style cabbage rolls filled with buckwheat groats, diced chicken, and finely chopped hard-boiled eggs. Kurpie is a region along the banks of the River Narew and its tributaries, in the Green Forest area northeast of Warsaw.

**gołąbki po staropolsku** Old Polish-style cabbage rolls stuffed with barley, chopped pork and wild mushrooms.

**gołąbki z grzybów i jaj** cabbage rolls stuffed with rice and finely chopped hard-boiled eggs.

**gołąbki z kaszą i grzybami** cabbage rolls filled with buckwheat groats and mushrooms.

**gołębie pieczone nadziewane** roasted stuffed squab.

**gotowane jajka** boiled eggs.

**NATIONAL FAVORITE** **groch purée** mashed yellow split peas with bits of bacon. A small mound of it typically accompanies a boiled pork shank (*golonka*).

**NATIONAL FAVORITE** **grochówka** yellow split pea soup; also called *zupa grochowa* or simply *grochowa*.

**grochówka myśliwska z boczkiem wędzonym** yellow split pea soup with smoked bacon, flavored with juniper.

**grochówka postna z grzybami** Lenten yellow split pea soup with mushrooms.

**groszek ptysiowy** small pastry puffs added to soups.

**groszek z marchewką** peas and carrots.

**groszek zielony zaprawiany żółtkami** peas with egg sauce.

**gruszki w czekoladzie** pears in chocolate sauce.

**gruszki w rumie** pears in rum.

**grzaniec z piwa** mulled beer.

**grzaniec z wina** mulled wine.

**grzanki ze szprotkami** toast with sprats (small, herring-like fish).

**GREAT** **grzany miód** mulled mead.

**grzybowa** mushroom soup; also called *zupa grzybowa*.

**grzyby marynowane** marinated mushrooms.

**grzyby panierowane** breaded mushrooms.

**grzyby w maśle** mushrooms in butter.

**grzyby ze smietaną** mushrooms in sour cream.

**gulasz barani** lamb goulash.

**gulasz wieprzowy z marchewką** pork goulash with carrots.

**gulasz wołowy** beef goulash.

**gulasz z gęsich podróbek** goose giblet goulash.

**TOP** *Amoniaki,* sugar-coated sour cream cookies made with an unusual leavening agent, ammonium carbonate. **MIDDLE** *Golonka* (pork hocks), the signature dish of the Kubicki restaurant in the Old Town section of Gdańsk in northern Poland. **BOTTOM** Fanciful breads in the shape of animals, created at the Sarzyński bakery in the picturesque town of Kazimierz Dolny, about 75 miles southeast of Warsaw.

**TOP LEFT** Early morning vendor selling Cracow's favorite street food, poppyseed-coated, ring-shaped rolls called *obwarzanki krakowskie*. **TOP RIGHT** Women doing a brisk business selling farmer's cheese in the Kleparski Central Market Plaza in Cracow. **BOTTOM** Karczma u Piotra, a roadside eatery (*karczma*) in southern Poland, near Lubien, on the way to Zakopane.

**TOP** *Ser owczy zapiekany,* a dish of smoked sheep's cheese (*oszczypek*) made in the Tatra Mountain region in southern Poland, served at the Chimera restaurant in Cracow. **MIDDLE** Fruit and vegetable market at the Plac Wielkopolski in Poźnan in western Poland. **BOTTOM** *Naleśniki po lwowsku,* Lwów-style crêpes filled with a seasoned potato mixture, served at the Lwowska restaurant in Wrocław in southwestern Poland. The formerly Polish city of Lwów (now Lviv) is in western Ukraine, having been incorporated into the Soviet Union after World War II.

**TOP LEFT** *Moskol pański,* a bread-like potato pancake topped with ham, mushrooms and grated cheese. It is a specialty of the Podhale region in southern Poland. **TOP RIGHT** A basket of *oczszypek,* sheep's cheese from the Tatra Mountains in southern Poland. **MIDDLE** Large loaf of whole-grain peasant bread at the outdoor museum (*skansen*) at Sierpc in western Poland. **BOTTOM** *Kaczka gdańska,* Gdańsk-style duck with a baked apple stuffed with cabbage, served at the Pod Łososiem restaurant in Gdańsk in northern Poland.

**TOP LEFT** First course of the day's main meal (*obiad*) in the small village of Baryczka in southeastern Poland. Homemade noodles are set out in bowls, waiting for broth to be poured onto them as soon as diners are seated. **TOP RIGHT** Inviting display of tomatoes in the fruit and vegetable market at the Plac Wielkopolski in Poznań in western Poland. **BOTTOM LEFT** Strings of dried "king bolete" mushrooms (*borowiki*) hanging at the outdoor market in Rzeszów in southeastern Poland. **BOTTOM RIGHT** Some of the many salads and appetizers awaiting hungry eaters at the Flik restaurant in Warsaw.

**TOP LEFT** Creamy kohlrabi soup with chives, a nouvelle approach to Polish cuisine by Bernard Lussiana **TOP RIGHT**, executive chef at Le Royal Meridien Bristol in Warsaw. **MIDDLE** Fruits and vegetables at Hala Targowa, the huge indoor market at Wrocław in southwestern Poland. **BOTTOM** Apple tart (*szarlotka*) and crêpe (*naleśnik*) at the Wierszynek restaurant in Cracow.

**TOP LEFT** *Chłodnik,* a cold, summertime soup with young beets and beet greens, served at a roadside eatery (Karczma u Fela), in southeastern Poland near Zamość. **MIDDLE LEFT** Gingerbread made by the famous Kopernik bakery in Toruń in western Poland. **RIGHT** Maciej Kuroń, popular TV chef and owner of the Studio Buffo restaurant in Warsaw. **BOTTOM** Breaded and fried walleyed pike (*sandacz*), a specialty of the Retman restaurant, which is housed in an old Hanseatic burgher's house in the Old Town area of Gdańsk in northern Poland.

**TOP** *Sernik przekladany,* a layered cheesecake. The outside layers of cake, one of which is colored and flavored with cocoa, are separated by a layer of cheesecake. **MIDDLE** A dish of wild boar with hunter's sauce accompanied by buckwheat groats, served at the Zajazd Staropolski restaurant in Toruń in western Poland. **BOTTOM** Some of the many varieties of Polish sausage (*kiełbasa*) in a grocery store in Toruń.

**gulasz z sarniny** venison goulash.

**gulasz z serc wieprzowych** pork heart goulash.

**hałuski z mlekiem** boiled dumplings made with uncooked, grated potatoes, eaten with hot milk.

**hałuski ze skwarkami** unfilled potato pasta with cracklings on top; it is a regional specialty of the Tatra Mountain region in southern Poland.   **REGIONAL CLASSIC**

**herbata** tea.

**herbata góralska ze spirytusem** highlander tea with spirits.

**herbata korzenna** spiced tea.

**herbata z miodem** tea with honey.   **GOOD CHOICE**

**hreczuszki** buckwheat pancakes.

**indyk w sosie maderowym** turkey in Madeira sauce.

**indyk zapiekany z kluskami** turkey and noodle casserole.

**jabłka na winie czerwonym** baked apples with red wine.

**jabłka w cieście** apple fritters.

**jabłko pieczone** baked apple.

**jabłko w cieście francuskim** apple in puff pastry.

**jabło drwali** two hefty potato pancakes with goulash sandwiched   **REGIONAL CLASSIC**
between them. It is a regional dish from the Żywiec region of southern Poland.

**jabłuszka w cieście** apple slices coated with batter, fried and sprinkled with powdered sugar.

**jaja faszerowane na gorąco** hot stuffed eggs. Unpeeled hard-   **NATIONAL FAVORITE**
boiled eggs are cut in two lengthwise. The egg is gently scooped out of the shell, finely chopped, mixed with seasoning and minced chives and parsley, and returned to the shells. Filled shells are sprinkled with breadcrumbs, turned top side down and lightly browned in butter. See recipe, p. 41.

**jaja na grzankach** baked eggs on toast.

jaja na miękko  soft-boiled eggs.

jaja na twardo  hard-boiled eggs.

jaja sadzone na szynce  fried eggs on ham.

jaja sadzone w śmietanie  eggs coddled in sour cream.

jaja w koszulkach  poached eggs.

jaja w szklance po polsku  Polish-style soft-boiled egg cooked in a drinking glass set in a pan of simmering water.

jaja z boczkiem  bacon and eggs.

jaja z sosem szczawiowym  eggs with sorrel sauce.

jajecznica  scrambled eggs.

**DELICIOUS**  jajecznica bosmańska  scrambled eggs with a steak wrapped around a mixture of mushrooms and chopped parsley to form a ball, which is then coated with small croutons.

**REGIONAL CLASSIC**  jajecznica na solonej gęsinie  scrambled eggs with salt-cured goose. It is a Kurpie dish.

**REGIONAL CLASSIC**  jajecznica po bacowsku  shepherd-style scrambled eggs with sautéed black bread cubes and smoked sheep's milk cheese. This a regional specialty of the Tatra Mountain area in southern Poland.

**REGIONAL CLASSIC**  jajecznica ze śledziem  scrambled eggs with herring, a specialty of the Kashubian area; served cold.

jajka faszerowane z sosem  stuffed eggs with sauce; served cold.

jajka na boczku  bacon and eggs.

jajka po wiedeńsku  Viennese-style soft-boiled eggs with butter.

jajka sadzone  fried eggs, sunny side up.

jajka w auszpiku  eggs in aspic; served cold.

jajka w koszulkach  poached eggs.

jajka w sosie chrzanowym  eggs in horseradish sauce; served cold.

jajka w sosie musztardowym  eggs in mustard sauce; served cold.

**GOOD CHOICE**  jajka z sardelkami  hard-boiled eggs sliced in half. Each is topped with anchovy fillets placed to form an "X;" served cold.

jajka z szynką w galarecie  eggs with ham in aspic; served cold.

jajka zawijane w szynce  hard-boiled eggs rolled-up in ham slices; served cold.

jarzyny duszone  braised vegetables.

jarzyny faszerowane  stuffed vegetables.

**NATIONAL FAVORITE**  jarzyny po polsku  vegetables Polonaise (topped with buttered breadcrumbs).

jesiotr w sosie kawiorowym  sturgeon in caviar sauce.

jusznik  duck or goose blood soup also called *czernina*.

**kaczka duszona w sosie kaparowym** braised duck in caper sauce.

**kaczka duszona z czerwoną kapustą** braised duck in red cabbage.

**kaczka duszona z oliwkami** braised duck in wine sauce with olives.

**kaczka gdańska** Gdańsk-style roasted duck with oranges served with a baked apple stuffed with red cabbage. See color insert, p. 4. The port city of Gdańsk is the biggest city in northern Poland, in the region of Pomerania. **REGIONAL CLASSIC**

**kaczka na musie jabłkowym** duck on apple purée.

**kaczka nadziewana cielęciną** roasted duck stuffed with veal.

**kaczka pieczona z jabłkami** roasted duck stuffed with apples. See recipe, p. 52. **NATIONAL FAVORITE**

**kaczka w galarecie** duck in aspic.

**kaczka z jabłkami** duck with apples.

**kaczka z wiśniami** roasted duck with cherries.

**kalaflor po polsku** cooked cauliflower topped with breadcrumbs browned in butter. See recipe, p. 54. **NATIONAL FAVORITE**

**kalarepa faszerowana** stuffed kohlrabi.

**kalteszal** cold, sweet-sour beer soup with egg yolks, cinnamon, sugar, lemon juice, rum and raisins.

**kanapki z pasztetem** canapés of pâté.

**kapłon nadziewany szynką** capon stuffed with ham.

**kapłon pieczony** roasted capon.

**kapłon z kremem z pieca** roasted capon in a sour cream sauce.

**kapusta kiszona** sauerkraut; also called *kapusta kwaszona.* **NATIONAL FAVORITE**

**kapusta kiszona na winie** sauerkraut in wine.

**kapusta kiszona zasmażana** sauerkraut browned in flour and butter.

**kapusta z grochem** sauerkraut with dried peas.

**kapusta z grzybami** sauerkraut with mushrooms.

**kapusta z wieprzowiną** sauerkraut with pork.

**kapuśniak** soup made with sauerkraut or fresh cabbage. **NATIONAL FAVORITE**

**kapuśniak z białej kapusty** white (green) cabbage soup.

**kapuśniak z kiszonej kapusty** sauerkraut soup.

**kapuśniak zabielany** creamed cabbage soup.

**karasie duszone z chrzanem** crappies in horseradish.

**karczochy faszerowane** stuffed artichokes.

**karczochy na winie** artichokes in wine.

**karkówka z dzika w sosie jałowcowyn** wild boar's neck with juniper sauce.

**karmonadel** pounded and breaded pork cutlets.

NATIONAL FAVORITE **karp królewski z prawdziwkami w wiejskiej śmietanie** royal carp with king bolete mushrooms cooked in country-style sour cream sauce.

**karp na słodko z migdałami** carp in sweet almond sauce.

**karp nadziewany** stuffed carp.

**karp nadziewany sardelami** carp stuffed with anchovies.

**karp nadziewany w cieście** whole stuffed carp encased in dough.

**karp po grecku** Greek-style cold carp in onion and tomato sauce.

NATIONAL FAVORITE **karp po żydowsku** Jewish-style poached carp steaks cooked in a caramel sauce with raisins, cloves and almonds.

**karp smażony** fried carp.

**karp w galarecie** carp in aspic.

NATIONAL FAVORITE **karpatka** craggy-topped cake made with puff pastry dough, which is named for the Carpathian Mountains. It is filled with pudding and dusted with powdered sugar so the surface peaks look like snow-covered mountains.

REGIONAL CLASSIC **kartacze** large, oval, meat-filled dumplings made with potatoes and potato flour. It is typical of Poland's eastern borderlands.

**kartofelki sauté** sautéed potatoes.

**kartoflane kluski** potato dumplings.

**kartofle chrupiące** French fries; also called *frytki*.

**kartofle duszone wyborne** scalloped potatoes.

**kartofle duszone ze śmietaną** potatoes smothered in sour cream.

**kartofle gotowane** boiled potatoes.

**kartofle pieczone** baked potatoes.

**kartofle smażone** fried potatoes.

NATIONAL FAVORITE **kartofle tłuczone** whipped or mashed potatoes; also called *kartofle purée*. Often, the potatoes are served on a platter in small, individual-size mounds topped with cracklings or bacon and chopped chives.

**kartofle w mundurkach** baked potatoes.

DELICIOUS **kartofle wiejskie** country-style mashed potatoes with cracklings or bits of bacon.

**kartofle wypiekane z jajami i śledziem** baked potato casserole with eggs and herring.

**kartofle z serem** potatoes with small chunks of farmer's cheese.

**kartofle z wody** boiled potatoes.

**kasza z serem** groats with small chunks of farmer's cheese.

**kaszanka zapiekana w boczku** casserole of blood sausage with bacon.

**kasztany osmażane w cukrze** candied chestnuts.

**katarzynka** chocolate-covered gingerbread cookie; also called *pierniczki w czekoladzie* or just *pierniczki*. NATIONAL FAVORITE

**kiełbasa duszona z młodą kapustą** stewed sausage and new cabbage.

**kiełbasa jałowcowa** juniper-smoked *kiełbasa*.

**kiełbasa w polskim sosie** sausage in Polish sweet-sour sauce.

**kiełbasa z czerwoną kapustą** sausage with red cabbage.

**kiełbasa z fasolką szparagową** sausage with wax beans.

**kisiel z żurawin** jelly-like cranberry dessert.

**kleik** gruel made with barley or whole-wheat groats.

**klops** meat loaf; also called *pieczeń rzymski*.

**klops nadziewany kaszą** meat loaf made by spreading buckwheat grits on a layer of ground meat and rolling it up like a jelly roll.

**klopsiki** meatballs.

**klopsiki cielęce duszone** stewed veal meatballs.

**klopsiki w śmietanie** meatballs in sour cream.

**kluski kartoflane** potato dumplings made by cutting long, approximately half-inch thick rolls of potato dough into about two-inch pieces, and cooking them in boiling water. They are topped with cracklings or bacon bits. Another name for these dumplings is *kopytki*. See recipe, p. 54. NATIONAL FAVORITE

**kluski kładzione** small egg-batter dumplings served in non-clear soups.

**kluski śląskie** Silesian dumplings made with mashed potatoes and potato flour. They have a central dimple in them made with a finger. Silesia (Śląsk) occupies the southwestern region of Poland. REGIONAL CLASSIC

**kluski wątrobiane** liver dumplings.

**kluski zapiekane** baked noodles with cheese.

**kluski z grzybami** mushroom dumplings.

**kluski z makiem i rodzynkami** egg noodles with poppy seeds and raisins. It is part of the traditional Christmas Eve meal (*wigilia*). NATIONAL FAVORITE

**kluski z serem** noodles with small chunks of farmer's cheese.

**knedle drobiowe w sosie koperkowyn** chicken dumplings in dill sauce.

**knedle ze śliwkami** potato dumplings filled with plums. FABULOUS

**knelki** quenelles, small oblong pieces of a finely chopped meat or fish mixture, boiled and served with a sauce or as a garnish.

NATIONAL FAVORITE **kolacky** cookies with a daub of jam placed in an indentation made on the surface.

**kołacz** coffee cake made like a jelly roll, filled with nuts, fruit and fruit peels, then formed into a ring by bringing ends together.

**kołaczki** small nut- or fruit-filled rolls.

NATIONAL FAVORITE **kołduny** small, round or semicircular pastas filled with either mutton and suet, or mushrooms, which are boiled and served in soup. To make round ones, a large circle of dough is topped with small mounds of filling placed a few inches apart from one another. On top of all of this is placed another large circle of dough. Individual, small circles are cut out with a round cookie cutter or small glass centered over each mound and the cut edges are sealed by pinching them together. Half-round ones are made by cutting out individual, small circles of dough and putting a small mound of meat off center on each. The uncovered half is folded over the filled half and the edges are sealed. *Kołduny* is the Lithuanian name for *pierogi*. The dish is also called *kołduny litewskie,* meaning Lithuanian-style. Not surprisingly, several Lithuanian dishes have become part of the Polish culinary repertoire as a result of the Polish-Lithuanian union that began in the late 14th century and lasted 400 years.

**kompot mieszany** mixed compote.

**kompot z gruszek** pear compote.

**kompot z jabłek** apple compote.

**kompot z pigw** quince compote.

**kompot z rabarbaru** rhubarb compote.

**kopytki** potato dumplings; see also *kluski kartoflane,* this *Guide.*

**kopytki z kapustą zasmażaną** potato dumplings with fried cabbage.

GREAT **kotlet bozmański** minced meat wrapped around a mixture of mushrooms, breadcrumbs and parsley to form a ball, which is coated with small croutons and deep-fried. See recipe, p. 51.

**kotlet cielęcy z pieczarkami** veal chop with mushrooms.

**kotlet de volaille** breaded, fried chicken fillet wrapped around butter.

**kotlet jarski** veggie patty or burger.

**kotlet mielony** meat patty or hamburger. Also called *kotlet siekany.*

GOOD CHOICE **kotlet sautée w sosie myśliwskim** pork cutlet in juniper-flavored hunter's sauce.

**kotlety bite z pulardy** pounded chicken breast cutlets.

**kotlety cielęce panierowane** breaded veal chops.

**kotlety schabowe** breaded pork cutlets. They typically are served with sauerkraut and boiled potatoes, a combination platter that is very popular. NATIONAL FAVORITE

**kotlety wieprzowe duszone** braised pork chops.

**kotlety wieprzowe z kostką** breaded pork chops.

**kotlety z fasoli** bean cutlets or patties.

**kotlety z grzybów** mushroom cutlets or patties.

**kotlety z móżdżku cielęcego** calf's brain cutlets.

**kotlety z ryb** fish cutlets.

**kotlety ziemniaczane** fried potato cutlets made from mashed or grated cooked potatoes mixed with egg and flour.

**krem selerowy z groszkiem ptysiowym** cream of celery soup garnished with tiny pastry puffs.

**krem warzywny** creamy puréed vegetable soup.

**krem z łososia** cream of salmon soup.

**krem z pieczarek** cream of mushroom soup.

**krewetki w sosie pikantnym** prawns in spicy sauce.

**krokiety kartoflane** potato croquettes.

**krokiety naleśnikowe** croquettes made out of a crêpe spread with meat, mushroom or sauerkraut, then folded or rolled, dipped in beaten egg and breadcrumbs, and fried. DELICIOUS

**krokiety z ryb** fish croquettes.

**królik duszony z grzybami** rabbit stewed with mushrooms.

**królik duszony z śmietanie** rabbit leg with sour cream sauce.

**królik marynowany** marinated rabbit.

**kruchy placek ze śliwkami** plum cake made with flaky dough.

**krupnik polski** Polish-style vegetable and barley soup. NATIONAL FAVORITE

**krupnik z podróbkami** vegetable and barley soup with giblets.

**kulebiak z kapustą i grzybami** loaf-shaped pastry filled with cabbage and mushrooms.

**kura po królewsku** royal-style chicken in sour cream, sprinkled with paprika.

**kurczak à la flaczki** spicy dish of chicken cut into thin, inch-long strips to look like tripe.

**kurczak w sosie imbirowo-rodzynkowym** chicken in ginger and raisin sauce.

**kurczę pieczone** roasted chicken.

**kurczę z nadzieniem po polsku** Polish-style roasted chicken stuffed with a dill-seasoned mixture of bread and liver and/or ground meat. NATIONAL FAVORITE

**kurczę z nadzieniem rodzynkowym**  roasted chicken with raisin stuffing.

**kurczę z rożna**  chicken barbecued on a spit.

**kurczęta pieczone po polsku**  Polish-style roasted young chicken stuffed with a breadcrumb, dill and parsley stuffing.

**kurczęta po polsku**  Polish-style chicken stuffed with a mixture of chopped chicken livers, breadcrumbs, egg, dill and milk.

**kurczęta smażone**  fried chicken.

**kurki w śmietanie z koperkiem**  golden chanterelle mushrooms in sour cream and dill sauce.

**kuropatwy w polskim sosie**  partridges in Polish sauce.

**kurzy rosół**  chicken broth.

**kutia wigilijna**  a sweet, cold, vanilla-flavored dish of boiled wheat with honey, poppy seeds and raisins, served as a part of the traditional Christmas Eve dinner (*wigilia*) in southeastern Poland; also spelled *kucja*.

**kwas**  sweet-sour pork and prune soup enjoyed in the Poznań area; also called *kwaśne*.

**kwaśna zyntyca**  drink made of sour whey; it is popular in the Tatra Mountain area and Cracow.

**kwaśnica z ziemniakami**  sauerkraut soup with lamb and potatoes, flavored with caraway; it is a regional dish from the Tatra Mountain area of southern Poland.


**legumina chlebowa**  black bread pudding.

**legumina migdałowa**  baked almond pudding.

**leniwe pierogi**  "lazy" (unfilled) *pierogi* made with cheese-containing dough cut into bite-size pieces and boiled; also called *pierogi leniwe*.

**lin pieczony z farszem**  baked stuffed tench.

**lin smażony**  fried tench.


**łazanki z kapustą**  pasta squares with cabbage and bacon.

**łosoś w czerwonem winie**  salmon in red wine.

**łosoś w galarecie**  salmon in gelatin.

**łosoś wędzony**  smoked salmon.

**łuki**  crescent roll; also called *rogal*.

**maczanka po krakowsku** beef with caraway in bread. It is a specialty of Cracow.

**maczanka po lwowsku** Lwów-style pork neck meat served in a bun. The city of Lwów was in the eastern borderlands of Poland that were incorporated into the Soviet Union after World War II. It is now called L'viv, and is in western Ukraine close to the Polish border.

**majonez z ozora** tongue in mayonnaise.

**makagigi** poppy seed, almond and honey sweetmeats traditionally enjoyed at Christmas.　　　　　　　　　　　　　　　NATIONAL FAVORITE

**makaron ze smardzami** noodles with morels.

**makaroniki makowe** poppy seed macaroons.

**makowiec** poppy seed roll. A filling of finely ground poppy seeds 　NATIONAL FAVORITE
mixed with honey, raisins, nuts and vanilla is spread on yeast dough and the dough is then rolled up into a jelly roll and baked. It traditionally is served on Christmas Eve. Other names for this dessert are *makownik* and *strucla z makiem*.

**marchew krajana ze szparagami** sliced carrots with asparagus.

**marchew po mazursku** Masur-style carrots cooked in a cream 　REGIONAL CLASSIC
sauce flavored with dill. Masuria (Mazury in Polish) is a region in northeastern Poland.

**marchew smażona** fried carrots.

**marchewka po polsku** Polish-style carrots topped with browned, buttered breadcrumbs.

**marcinki** crescent rolls filled with a mixture of white poppy seeds. It traditionally is eaten at the beginning of Advent on St. Martin's day in the western Poznań region.

**marynowana baranina** marinated mutton.

**mazurek daktylowy** flat cake with dates and other candied fruits.

**mazurek królewski** royal-style flat cake made of dough with sieved egg yolks. A latticework of icing is drizzled on top.

**mazurek orzechowy** flat cake with ground walnuts. See recipe, p. 59.　WONDERFUL

**mazurek pomarańczowy** flat cake with candied orange peel.

**metka** soft, uncooked sausage from the Poznań area, which is 　REGIONAL CLASSIC
spread on bread.

**mieszanka warzywna** mixed vegetables.

**migdały palone** roasted almonds.

**miodownik** honey-spice cake, gingerbread. Also called *piernik*.

**mizeria** thinly sliced cucumbers in sour cream dressing. See 　NATIONAL FAVORITE
recipe, p. 50.

**mleczko waniliowe** vanilla custard.

**morszczuk panierowany** breaded grenadier fish.

**REGIONAL CLASSIC** **moskol juhaski** bread-like potato pancake topped with butter and *kefir,* a yogurt-like milk product. It is a specialty of the Podhale region.

**REGIONAL CLASSIC** **moskol pański** bread-like potato pancake topped with ham, mushrooms and grated cheese; it is a specialty of the Podhale region. See color insert, p. 2.

**mostek barani faszerowany** stuffed breast of mutton.

**DELICIOUS** **mostek cielęcy nadziewany** stuffed veal breast.

**mostek nadziewany wątróbką** veal breast with liver stuffing.

**móżdżki wieprzowe** pork brains.

**móżdżki wołowe w białym sosie** beef brains in white sauce.

**muchomorki** garnishes made to look like mushrooms. The stem is a hard-boiled egg with the ends cut off and the cap is an overturned tomato half, with a dollop of mayonnaise on it.

**nadziewana pieczona ryba** stuffed baked fish.

**nadziewane ciastka** jelly-roll–like fruit rolls, cut at an angle in one-inch pieces.

**nadziewany indyk** stuffed turkey.

**REGIONAL CLASSIC** **naleśniki po lwowsku** Lwów-style crêpes stuffed with a seasoned potato mixture. The city of Lwów was in the eastern border-lands of Poland that were incorporated into the Soviet Union after World War II. It is now called L'viv, and is in western Ukraine, very close to the Polish border. See color insert, p. 3.

**naleśniki z dżemem** crêpes with jam.

**naleśniki z nadzieniem jagodowym i smietaną** crêpes with berries and sour cream.

**naleśniki z owocami** crêpes with fruit.

**napoleonka** puff pastry with pastry cream.

**nerka cielęca pieczona w klarowanym maśle** veal kidneys baked in clarified butter.

**nerkówka cielęca nadziewana** roast stuffed veal with kidney.

**nóżki cielęce smażone** fried calf's feet.

**REGIONAL CLASSIC** **nugat lwowski** Lwów-style nougat. The nougat is sandwiched between wafer sheets.

ogórki faszerowane na zimno cold, stuffed cucumbers.

omlet z cynaderkami omelette with kidneys.

omlet z dżemem omelette with jam.

omlet z kurkami omelette with *kurka,* the golden chanterelle mushroom.

owoce kompotowe w spirytusie fruit compote in spirits.

owocowa z kluskami fruit soup with noodles.

ozorki wieprzowe w sosie pomidorowym pork tongues in tomato sauce.

ozór w sosie chrzanowym tongue in horseradish sauce.

ozór wołowy po polsku w szarym sosie beef tongue in Polish   **NATIONAL FAVORITE**
gray sauce, a sauce made with browned flour, butter and broth, and almonds, raisins, wine and caramelized sugar.

paluszki drożdżowe yeast-raised stick crackers served with soups.

panas kaszubski Kashubian head cheese. Kashubia encompasses   **REGIONAL CLASSIC**
an area of about 70 miles southwest of the city of Gdańsk, in the region of Pomerania.

paprykarz Hungarian goulash; paprikash.

parówki na gorąco hot dogs, served hot.

pascha crustless Passover cheesecake, a traditional Easter dessert   **NATIONAL FAVORITE**
from eastern Poland attributed to Slavic Jews.

pasta z kurzej wątróbki chicken liver spread.

pasta z pieczarek mushroom spread.

pasztecik drożdżowy small soup pastries made with yeast dough.

pasztaciki postne small Lenten (meatless) pastries filled with   **GREAT**
mushrooms. See recipe for easy-to-make pastries, p. 48.

pasztaciki z mózgu small brain-filled pastries.

pasztaciki z raków small crayfish-filled pastries.

pasztet mięsny meat pâté.

pasztet wieprzowy pork pâté.

pasztet z bażanta z żurawina cold pheasant pie with cranberries.

pasztet z cielęciny veal pâté.

pasztet z dziczyzny venison pâté.   **TASTY**

pasztet z kurczęcia w cieście covered pie of chicken and mushrooms flavored with dill.

**pasztet z prosiaka** suckling pig pâté.

**pączki** filled, raised doughnut that is fried and usually glazed with icing or dusted with powdered sugar. Favorite fillings include plum/prune and rosehip preserves.

**perliczka nadziewana** roasted, stuffed guinea hen.

**pieczarki z patelni** fried, cultivated button mushrooms.

**pieczeń barania** roasted mutton.

**pieczeń barania faszerowana** stuffed roasted mutton.

**pieczeń barania z pieca** roasted leg of mutton.

**pieczeń cielęca** roasted veal.

**pieczeń cielęca nadziewana** stuffed veal roast.

**pieczeń cielęca w sosie tatarskim** sliced, cold roasted veal in tartar sauce.

**pieczeń huzarska** Hussar-style roast beef; the roast is cut into slices when tender and each slice is partially sliced again to form a pocket that is filled with a mixture of onion and breadcrumbs. The roast is then reassembled to form its original shape and cooked to heat the stuffing. Also called *pieczeń wołowa po husarsku.*

**pieczeń Radeckiego** round steak sliced to form a pocket that is filled with lemon slices and a mixture of breadcrumbs, egg yolks and horseradish. The filled meat is then rolled up, tied and cooked in a cream sauce.

**pieczeń rzymski** meat loaf; also called *klops.*

**pieczeń rzymski w sosie śmietanowym** sliced meat loaf in sour cream sauce.

**pieczeń wieprzowa duszona w jarzynach** roasted pork in a vegetable sauce.

**pieczeń wieprzowa w kiszonej kapuście** roasted pork and sauerkraut.

**pieczeń wieprzowa z szynki** roasted fresh ham.

**pieczeń wołowa duszona** beef pot roast.

**pieczeń wołowa na dziko** mock venison pot roast made with beef marinated in sauce containing juniper berries typically used for game.

**pieczeń wołowa po husarsku** see *pieczeń huzarska.*

**pieczeń wołowa z grzybami** roasted beef with mushrooms.

**pieczeń wołowa z pieczarkami** roasted beef with cultivated button mushrooms.

**pieczeń z duszonymi ogórkami** pot roast with cucumbers.

**pieczeń z dzika** roasted wild boar.

**pieczeń z indyka z żurawiną** roasted turkey with cranberries.

**pieczeń z łosia** roasted moose.

**pieczeń z rożna** meat roasted on a spit.

**pierniczki w czekoladzie** little honey-spice cakes covered with chocolate; also called *katarzynka*.

**piernik** honey-spice cake, gingerbread. Also called *miodownik*.

**piernik toruński** honey-spice cake from Toruń, a port city on the lower Vistula River in Pomerania. Gingerbread has been made there since medieval times. See color insert, p. 7.

**piernik wyborny** honey-spice cake with fruit.

**pierogi** thin circles of pasta dough topped on one side with sweet or savory fillings, then folded in half, sealed at the edges and boiled. Meat, sauerkraut, potatoes, cheese and fruit are typical fillings.

**pierogi leniwe** "lazy" (unfilled) *pierogi* made with cheese-containing dough cut into bite-size pieces and boiled; also called *leniwe pierogi*.

**pierogi łomnickie** rye flour and potato *pierogi* filled with *bryndza*—salty, white sheep's cheese—then boiled and served with butter on top. It is named after the small village of Łomnica in the Tatra Mountains in southern Poland.

**pierogi ruskie** *pierogi* filled with a mixture of cheese and potatoes. This type of *pierogi* originated long ago in the eastern Polish borderlands (Ruthenia). It is also called *pierogi z kartoflami i serem*.

**pierogi smażone** fried *pierogi*.

**pierogi z jagodami** *pierogi* filled with blueberries.

**pierogi z kapustą i grzybami** *pierogi* filled with sauerkraut and mushrooms.

**pierogi z kartoflami i serem** see *pierogi ruskie*.

**pierogi z mięsem** meat-stuffed *pierogi*.

**pierożki** yeast-raised *pierogi* that are baked rather than boiled in water; also called *pierogi drożdżowe*.

**pieróg gryczany** loaf of buckwheat groats, cheese and potatoes baked in dough. Also called *pieróg lubelski*. Lublin is a city southeast of Warsaw.

**piersi z perliczki w sosie z winogron** breast of guinea fowl in grape sauce.

**pierś indyka z kasztanami** turkey breast with chestnuts.

EXCELLENT

REGIONAL CLASSIC

NATIONAL FAVORITE

GOOD CHOICE

REGIONAL CLASSIC

**pierś z kaczki w sosie różanym** duck breast in rose-flavored sauce.

**piwo z miodem** honey beer.

**placek drożdżowy z kruszonką** yeast-raised crumb cake.

**placek z suszonych śliwek** prune tart.

**placek zbójnicki z gulaszem i surówkami** potato pancakes with beef stew and mixed salad.

**placek ze smardzami** savory flat cake topped with morels in aspic flavored with Madeira wine.

**placek ze śliwkami** plum cake.

*NATIONAL FAVORITE* **placki kartoflane** potato pancakes; also called *placki ziemniaczane*.

**placki kartoflane z boczkiem** potato pancakes with bacon.

*REGIONAL CLASSIC* **placki ziemniaczane po mazowiecku** Mazovian-style potato pancakes with sour cream. Mazovia is centrally located in the eastern half of Poland. This region includes Warsaw.

**płatki owsiane** oatmeal porridge.

**płucka cielęce z winem** calf's lungs in wine sauce.

**poemat** soft, unbaked cheesecake made from homemade cheese.

**polewka piwna z kminkiem** beer soup with caraway.

**polewka z piwa** soup made with beer, sour cream and beaten egg yolks, flavored with cinnamon.

*TASTY* **polewka z serwatki** cheese soup made with whey and fresh cheese curds, served with potatoes. It is a specialty of Galicia, which is the name given to the partition of Poland that was occupied by the Austrians from 1772 and 1918. See recipe, p. 47.

**polewka z wina** soup made with wine, beaten egg yolks and sugar, flavored with cinnamon, cloves and allspice.

**polędwica duszona ze śmietaną** tenderloin smothered in sour cream.

**pomidory faszerowane** stuffed tomatoes.

**pomidory faszerowane mięsem** tomatoes with meat stuffing.

**pomidory pieczone** baked tomatoes.

**pory z wody** boiled leek.

**potrawka barania z ogórkami** braised mutton with pickles.

*GREAT* **potrawka cielęca po staropolsku** Old Polish-style veal stewed with prunes and raisins.

**potrawka cielęca z jabłkami** veal stewed with apples.

**potrawka cielęca z jarzynami** veal stewed with vegetables.

**potrawka z baraniny** mutton fricassee.

**potrawka z kapłona z ryżem** casserole with capon and rice.

**potrawka z kurcząt po polsku** Polish-style quartered chicken with mushrooms in a wine and egg yolk sauce.

**potrawka z kury** chicken fricassee.

**potrawka z ogona** oxtail ragout.

**potrawka z polędwicy** beef tenderloin with onions.

**potrawka z zająca** hare fricassee.

**poziomkowy sos** wild strawberry sauce.

**półmisek sąsiedzki** cold meat platter.

**półmisek serów** cheese platter.

**półmisek serów bacowski** shepherd's plate of sheep's milk cheese    REGIONAL CLASSIC
with bread and butter; it is a regional specialty of the Tatra Mountain area of southern Poland.

**prosię nadziewane** stuffed piglet.

**prosię pieczone** roasted suckling pig.

**proziaki** peasant bread. See recipe, p. 60.    DELICIOUS

**przekładaniec** loaf cake with dried fruit filling.

**przekładaniec jabłkowy** coffee cake with apple filling.

**przepiórki z pieczarkami** quail with cultivated button mushrooms.

**pstrąg po podhalańsku** Podhale-style fried trout coated with    REGIONAL CLASSIC
melted sheep's cheese.

**pstrąg w galarecie** trout in aspic.    NATIONAL FAVORITE

**pstrąg z wody** poached trout.

**pstrągi marynowane** marinated trout.

**puchar ambrozja** sundae made with vanilla, chocolate and fruit-flavored ice cream topped with mixed fresh fruits, whipped cream, nuts and grated chocolate.

**puchar lodowy z owocami** sundae made with a variety of ice cream flavors with fruit.

**puchar lódow** ice cream sundae with various choices of flavors and toppings.

**pularda pieczona z sardelami** chicken with anchovies.

**pulpety nadziewane jajkami przepiórki w zurku** meatballs stuffed    GOOD CHOICE
with quail eggs in *żurek,* a sour ryemeal soup. See recipe, p. 45.

**pulpety z mózgu** calf's brain dumplings or balls.

**pulpety z ryb** fish dumplings or balls.

**pyry w mundurkach z gzikiem** potatoes in skins with cottage    REGIONAL CLASSIC
cheese, a regional dish of the Poznań area.

**pyzy** potato dumplings.

**DELICIOUS**    **racuchy** sour milk pancakes.

**racuszki z jabłkami** sour milk pancakes with grated apple.

**raki po polsku w śmietanie** Polish-style crayfish in sour cream, breadcrumbs and dill.

**risi-bisi** rice and peas.

**rogal** crescent roll; also called *łuki*.

**rogaliki drożdżowe** yeast-raised crescent roll.

**rolada cielęca** rolled, stuffed pounded veal, sliced and served cold.

**NATIONAL FAVORITE**    **rolada wieprzowa nadziewana kiełbasą** rolled pork loin stuffed with sausage.

**rolada z węgorza** roulade of eel.

**rolmops** rolled, marinated herring.

**rosół z ryby** fish broth.

**NATIONAL FAVORITE**    **rosół z wołowiny z kluskami lanemi** beef broth with egg-drop noodles. See recipe, p. 44.

**REGIONAL CLASSIC**    **rosół z zielonki gąski** broth with *gąski,* green-capped mushrooms. It is a specialty of the Kurpie region, which lies along the banks of the Narew river and its tributaries, in the Green Forest area northeast of Warsaw.

**rosól z żółtkiem** broth with raw egg yolk.

**rozbratel po chłopsku** peasant-style beef, sliced and rolled around a filling.

**rozbratel z cebulką** rib steak with onions.

**NATIONAL FAVORITE**    **róże karnawałowe** traditional pre-Lenten carnival rosettes. They are made from three small circles of dough of different diameters pressed together at their centers, with the largest one on the bottom and smallest on top. A few small cuts are made at the edge of each circle, which allows the dough to curve and appear petal-like when fried. Usually some jam or a cherry is then put into the center.

**ryba po grecku** Greek-style fish fillets cooked in a sweet-sour, tomato-based sauce with vegetables, served cold.

**ryba w galarecie** fish in aspic.

**ryba w sosie chrzanowym** fish fillets in horseradish sauce, served cold.

**ryba zapiekana** baked fish.

**rydze smażone** fried milky cap mushrooms.

**rzepa duszona z kiełbaskami** braised turnips with sausage.

**sałata łąkowa** field salad of lovage (*lubczyk*), nettles (*pokrzywa*) and sorrel (*szczaw*).

**sałatka bacowska** shepherd's salad with vegetables, sheep's cheese, pickles and tomatoes. It is a specialty of the Tatra Mountain area in southern Poland. REGIONAL CLASSIC

**sałatka kartoflana z winem** potato salad with wine.

**sałatka szefa kuchni** chef's salad. See recipe, p. 49.

**sałatka warszawska** Warsaw-style salad of beets, beans, peas, pickles and crabmeat in a mayonnaise, sour cream and mustard dressing. REGIONNAL CLASSIC

**sałatka z buraków z jajami** beet and egg salad.

**sałatka z czerwonej kapusty** red cabbage salad.

**sałatka z kartofli** potato salad. See recipe, p. 51. NATIONAL FAVORITE

**sałatka z kartofli z sardelami** potato salad with anchovies.

**sałatka z kiszonej kapusty** sauerkraut salad.

**sałatka z owoców sezonowych** seasonal fruit salad.

**sałatka z pomidorów** fresh tomato salad.

**sałatka z ryb i krabów** rice and crabmeat salad.

**sałatka z rzodkwi** black radish salad.

**sałatka z selerów** celery root salad.

**sandacz à la Radziwiłł** walleyed pike à la Radziwill; steamed fish fillets on toast, covered with a sauce of wine, mushrooms, truffles and shrimp.

**sandacz na winie** walleyed pike in wine sauce.

**sandacz po polsku** Polish-style fillet of walleyed pike topped with a hard-boiled egg half and cream sauce. NATIONAL FAVORITE

**sarna duszona** stewed venison.

**schab pieczony** roasted pork loin.

**schab pieczony a kwaszonymi jabłkami** roasted pork loin with sour-cured apples.

**schab pieczony ze śliwkami** roasted pork loin stuffed with prunes, served with a sauce of red wine and stewed prunes.

**schab w migdałach** roasted pork loin with almonds.

**schabowa pieczeń** slice of roasted pork loin.

**ser owczy zapiekany** baked slices of sheep's cheese. See color insert, p. 3.

**serce wołowe w sosie** braised beef heart with sauce.

**sernik** cheesecake. See recipe, p. 55. NATIONAL FAVORITE

**DELICIOUS**    **sernik przekladany** layered cheesecake. See recipe, p. 56 and color insert, p. 8.

**sernik wiedeński** Viennese cheesecake, which has a bottom layer of pastry, a middle layer of cheese mixture and a topping of jam, cocoa and raisins.

**sernik wielkanocny** Easter cheesecake.

**serowiec** cake made with cottage cheese or cream cheese.

**sękacz** see *dziad,* this *Guide.*

**siekane zrazy** minced chops.

**TASTY**    **smalec** spread made with fat studded with onion and cracklings.

**smażone kotlety z piersi kury** fried chicken breast cutlets.

**sok malinowy** raspberry juice.

**sok pomarańczowy** orange juice.

**sok pomidorowy** tomato juice.

**EXCELLENT**    **sok z czarnej porzeczki** black currant juice.

**sola na białem winie** sole in white wine.

**REGIONAL CLASSIC**    **sola po gdańsku w sosie z krewetek** Gdańsk-style sole in shrimp sauce. The port city of Gdańsk is the biggest city in northern Poland, in the region of Pomerania.

**sola z jarzynami** sole with vegetables.

**sola zapiekana z pomidorami** baked sole with tomato sauce.

**sos koperkowy** dill sauce.

**sos ostry** hot pepper sauce.

**sos z rumen** rum sauce.

**souflet owocowy** fruit soufflé.

**staropolska faramuszką** Old Polish-style creamy beer soup with caraway and small chunks of farmer's cheese.

**stek z jelenia** elk steak.

**NATIONAL FAVORITE**    **strucla makowa** poppy seed roll. A filling of finely ground poppy seeds mixed with honey, raisins, nuts and vanilla is spread on yeast dough and the dough is then rolled up into a jelly roll and baked. It traditionally is served on Christmas Eve. Other names for this dessert are *strucla z makiem, makownik* and *makowiec.*

**studzienina** see *galaretka z nóżek.*

**surówka z kiszonej kapusty** sauerkraut salad with carrots and apples.

**szare kluski** dumplings made with grated potatoes and flour; it is a specialty of Poznań.

**NATIONAL FAVORITE**    **szarlotka** Polish apple cake. See color insert, p. 6.

**szary sos staropolski** Old Polish gray sauce, historically a favorite sauce of Polish nobility. This sweet-sour sauce, which actually is brown, contains gingerbread, almonds, raisins, wine and caramelized sugar, and typically is served with poached fish or boiled beef tongue.

**szaszłyk barani** mutton shish kebab.

**szaszłyk z kurzych wątróbek** chicken liver shish kebab.

**szaszłyk z polędwicy** beef tenderloin shish kebab.

**szaszłyki wołowe** beef shish kebabs.

**szczaw** sorrel soup; also called *zupa szczawiowa* or *szczawiowa*. NATIONAL FAVORITE

**szczawiowa z jajkiem** sorrel soup with egg.

**szczupak duszony** stewed whole pike smothered in vegetables.

**szczupak po polsku** Polish-style pike with horseradish sauce or topped with a mixture of chopped eggs and dill in lemon juice.

**szczupak po węgiersku** Hungarian-style pike dusted with paprika and simmered in wine and broth.

**szczupak po żydowsku** Jewish-style steamed, stuffed pike. This NATIONAL FAVORITE elaborate dish requires that the skin, with tail attached, be separated from the flesh, which is cut-up, seasoned and then stuffed back into the skin.

**sznycel cielęcy po wiedeńsku** Viennese-style breaded veal cutlets.

**sznycel cielęcy z sardelami** breaded veal cutlets with anchovies.

**szparagi w sosie rakowym** asparagus in crayfish sauce.

**szpinak z czosnkiem** spinach with garlic.

**szpinak ze śmietanką** spinach with sweet cream.

**sztuka mięsa** boiled beef.

**sztuka mięsa w jarzynach** boiled beef with vegetables.

**szyjki gęsie nadziewane** deboned goose neck skin filled with GREAT stuffing.

**szynka gotowana** cooked ham.

**szynka gotowana na zimno** cold boiled ham.

**śledzie marynowane w śmietanie** pickled herring in sour cream.

**śledzie nadziewane** stuffed herring.

**śledź w oleju** herring in oil. NATIONAL FAVORITE

**śledź tatarski z majerankiem** herring tartare flavored with marjoram. ELEGANT See recipe, p. 39.

**ślimaki nadziewane** stuffed snails.

# MENU GUIDE

**ślimaki z pieczarkami** snails with button mushrooms.

**śliwki migdałowe** prunes filled with almonds and deep fried in batter, then rolled in sugar.

**świderki** sesame-coated twists.

GOOD CHOICE  **świeży łosoś bałtycki z dzikim ryżem** fresh Baltic salmon with wild rice.

**tatar z ogórkami** steak tartare with dill pickles.

**tłuczeńce** honey-rye wafers traditionally eaten at Christmas.

**tort bezowy** meringue torte.

**tort czekoladowy** chocolate torte.

**tort kawowy** mocha torte.

NATIONAL FAVORITE  **tort makowy** poppy seed torte.

**tort marcepanowy** marzipan torte.

**tort migdałowy** almond torte.

**tort orzechowy** nut torte.

**tort serowy w czekoladzie** cheese tort with chocolate.

**torty owocowe** fruit torte.

**tymbaliki z kaszy do zupy** timbales for soup made with *kasza krakowska,* the finest milled buckwheat.

NATIONAL FAVORITE  **tymbaliki z ryb** timbales of molded fish in aspic.

**tzimmes** sweet carrot dish of Jewish origin.

**udziec sarni na dziko** hunter's style leg of deer in juniper sauce.

**udziec z kozlęcia nadziewany czosnkiem i jajkiem** leg of goat stuffed with garlic and egg.

NATIONAL FAVORITE  **uszka** small pasta squares that have been folded over a mushroom filling to form a triangle and pinched together at two ends to form a ring. They traditionally are served in clear beet soup (*barszcz*) on Christmas Eve.

**vinaigrette** garden lettuce with oil and vinegar, often with sliced tomatoes; also spelled *winegret.*

**vinaigrette z żółtkiem** vinaigrette dressing with egg yolk.

**wątróbka cielęca sauté** sautéed calf's liver.  DELICIOUS

**wątróbka cielęca z jałowcem** calf's liver with juniper.

**wątróbka gęsia** goose liver spread.

**wątróbka po nelsońsku** liver and potato casserole with onions and mushrooms, simmered in Madeira or Sherry sauce. The dish is named for British Admiral Horatio Nelson.

**wątróbka wieprzowa panierowana** breaded pork liver.

**wątróbka z drobiu z jabłkami** chicken livers with apple.

**wątróbki z kur w sosie maderowym** chicken livers in Madeira sauce.

**węgorz pieczony** baked eel.

**węgorz wędzony** smoked eel.  NATIONAL FAVORITE

**węgorz zawijamy w boczku** eel wrapped in bacon.

**wiązanie pstrąga do gotowania** boiled whole trout, tethered head to tail to form a ring.

**wiejska kiełbasa** country-style smoked pork sausage with a light center and a dark outer edge.

**wieprzowina z gruszkami** pork and pears, a Silesian specialty.  REGIONAL CLASSIC

**winegret** garden lettuce with oil and vinegar, often with sliced tomatoes; also spelled *vinaigrette*.

**wołowina w chrzanem** beef with horseradish.


**zając po polsku ze śmietaną** Polish-style hare with sour cream.

**zając z sosem porzeczkowym** hare in currant sauce.

**zalewajka** potato soup.

**zapiekanka** half baguette topped with melted cheese and ketchup, a fast food item sold from street kiosks.

**zapiekanka z kiełbasą i kartoflami** layered casserole of sausage  REGIONAL CLASSIC and potatoes with sour cream, onions and hard-cooked eggs between the layers; it is a regional specialty of Rzeszów.

**zawijas z drobiu ze śliwką** pounded chicken breast roll-up with plum stuffing.

**zestaw warzywa** mixed salad.

**ziemniaki tłuczone** mashed potatoes.

**ziemniaki w mundurkach** potatoes cooked with the skin on.

**zimne mięsa** cold cuts.

**zimne nogi** jellied pig's knuckles or trotters; also known as *galareta z nóżek wieprzowych* and *studzienina*.

**zraziki cielęce** veal rolls.

**zrazy** beef roll-ups. See recipe, p. 53.

**zrazy à la Radziwiłł** pounded beef cutlets wrapped around a stuffing of bacon, mushrooms, pickle strips and sautéed onions, and served with sauce inside a small, hollowed-out loaf of dark bread.

**zrazy baranie** lamb rolls.

**zrazy cielęce zawijane po polsku** Polish-style veal roll-ups stuffed with an egg, breadcrumb and raisin mixture and served in a sour cream sauce.

**zrazy po nelsońsku** layered casserole of pounded tenderloin fillets, potatoes and mushrooms. The dish is named for British Admiral Horatio Nelson.

**zrazy siekane duszone** ground meat rolls.

**zrazy wołowe z pieczarkami** pounded beef roll-ups with cultivated button mushrooms.

**zrazy z grzybami i ze śmietaną** pounded beef roll-ups with mushrooms and sour cream.

**zrazy zawijane po warszawsku** Warsaw-style pounded beef roll-ups with onion breadcrumb stuffing.

**zupa chlebowa** beef broth–based bread soup with diced sausage topped with toast and a poached egg; another version is a milk-based soup made of puréed black bread and vegetables, subtly flavored with nutmeg.

**zupa chlebowa z biała kiełbasą** bread soup with fresh (not smoked) pork sausage.

**zupa cytrynowa z ryzem** lemon soup with rice.

**zupa dnia** soup of the day.

**zupa dyniowa** pumpkin soup.

**zupa fasolowa** bean soup.

**zupa grochowa** yellow split pea soup.

**zupa grochowa na wędzonce** yellow split pea and smoked ham soup.

**zupa grochowa przecierana** strained yellow split pea soup.

**zupa grzybowa** mushroom soup; also called simply *grzybowa;* after beet soup, this is the second-favorite soup served at supper on Christmas Eve.

**zupa grzybowa klarowna** clear mushroom soup.

**zupa grzybowa ze śmietaną** mushroom and sour cream soup.

**zupa jabłkowa** cold apple soup.

**zupa jagodowa** cold soup made with berries and cream, flavored with cinnamon or cloves. See recipe, p. 48.  **GREAT**

**zupa jagodowa czysta** clear berry soup.

**zupa jarzynowa** vegetable soup.

**zupa kalafiorowa** cauliflower soup.

**zupa kminkowa** caraway soup.

**zupa koperkowa** fresh dill soup.

**zupa migdałowa** almond soup.

**zupa mleczna z lanym ciastem** milk soup with egg noodles.

**zupa mleczna z płatkami kukurydzianymi** hot milk soup with corn flakes.

**zupa mleczna z ryżem** milk soup with rice.

**zupa nic** "nothing" soup; vanilla-flavored soup made with milk and whipped egg yolks, topped with small dollops of beaten egg whites briefly cooked in milk. It is eaten hot as a soup or cold as a dessert.  **NATIONAL FAVORITE**

**zupa ogonowa** oxtail soup.

**zupa ogórkowa** dill pickle soup. See recipe, p. 42.  **NATIONAL FAVORITE**

**zupa ogórkowa na barszczu** beet and cucumber soup.

**zupa owocowa** cold fruit soup.

**zupa pieczarkowa** mushroom soup made with cultivated button mushrooms.

**zupa piwna z serem** hot beer soup with cheese.

**zupa poziomkowa z winem** wild strawberry soup with wine.

**zupa rybna z pulpetami** fish ball soup.

**zupa rybne** creamy fish chowder, typically whitened with sour cream.

**zupa selerowa z grzankami** celery soup with croutons.

**zupa szczawiowa** sorrel soup; also called simply *szczaw*. See recipe, p. 47.  **NATIONAL FAVORITE**

**zupa wątrobiana** liver soup.

**zupa z cielęciny i ryżu** veal soup with rice.

**zupa z czernic** blueberry soup.

**zupa z flaczków** tripe soup.  **NATIONAL FAVORITE**

**zupa z kalarepy** kohlrabi soup.

**zupa z móżdżkiem** calf's brain soup.

**zupa z serwatki z ryżem** whey soup with rice.

**zupa z soczewicy** lentil soup.

**zupa z suszonych śliwek** prune and rhubarb soup flavored with cinnamon and cloves.

**zupa ze świeżych grzybów** fresh mushroom soup.

**zupa ziemniaczana** potato soup.

**żabki w potrawce** ragout of frog legs.

REGIONAL CLASSIC  **żagielek z ryby** cucumber stuffed with fish, a specialty of the Żywiec region in southern Poland.

**żeberka wędzone z grilla** grilled, smoked ribs.

**żeberka wieprzowe w kapuście** pork ribs with cabbage.

**żołądki kurze duszone** stewed chicken gizzards.

**żołądki w potrawce** chicken tripe fricassee.

NATIONAL FAVORITE  **żur** sour soup of fermented ryemeal; also called *żurek,* and in some parts of eastern Poland, *biały barszcz,* where it is made with rye bread, not rye flour.

**żur z kiełbasą** sour rye and cream soup with smoked sausage.

**żurek krakowski** Cracow-style ryemeal soup lightly flavored with marjoram and served on top of sliced hard-boiled eggs.

**żurek po dębicku** Dębica-style sour ryemeal soup served with hard-boiled eggs cut in half, and some mashed potatoes on the edge of the soup bowl. Dębica is a town east of Cracow in the region called Małopolska.

**żurek stryszewski** sour soup made with wheat. It is a specialty of the Żywiec region of southern Poland.

**żurek wielkanocny** special Easter soup made with sour oatmeal and ryemeal, boiled potatoes, sausage and hard-boiled eggs.

**żurek zakopiański** sour ryemeal soup with sausage, potatoes and mushrooms; it is a regional specialty of the Tatra Mountain region in southern Poland.

# Foods & Flavors Guide

This chapter is a comprehensive list of foods, spices, kitchen utensils and cooking terminology in Polish, with English translations. The list will be helpful in interpreting menus since it is impossible to cover all the flavors or combinations possible for certain dishes. It will also be useful for shopping in both supermarkets and the lively and fascinating outdoor markets.

**agrest** gooseberry.
**amoniak** ammonium carbonate, a type of baking powder.
**ananas** pineapple.
**antrykot** steak.
**anyż** anise.
**arbuz** watermelon; also called *kawon*.
**aronia** blueberry (cultivated).
**auszpik** aspic.
**awokado** avocado.

**baba** holiday and special-occasion sweet yeast cake made in a traditional, fluted tube pan that is wider than it is high and narrower on top. The cake's resemblance to the full skirts once worn by elderly peasant women (*baba,* singular) is said to be the reason why the cake bears its name. A smaller, similarly shaped cake is called *babka.* Some little, molded savory cakes are also called *babka* (see *Menu Guide*).
**babeczka** small roll, cupcake or tart.
**Baczewski** brand of vodka originally made in Lwów, a city in eastern Poland that was incorporated into Ukraine after World War II. Today this vodka is made in Wrocław, where many of the inhabitants of Lwów were relocated after the war.
**bakalie** warm-climate fruit and nuts, e.g., figs, raisins, dates and citrus fruit.
**bakłażan** eggplant.
**baleron** type of ham; it is boned, stuffed into a bladder, smoked and boiled.
**banan** banana.

**bar mleczny** milk bar offering cheap, meatless meals. This type of eatery, common during the communist era, is hard to find now. Also called *mleczarnia*.

**baranek** lamb; also called *jagnię* and *owieczka*.

**baranina** mutton; often used to mean lamb.

**bardzo mało wysmażone** food cooked very rare.

**barszcz** clear or creamy soup traditionally made with meat stock and *kwas*, the bright red, sour liquid obtained from fermented beets. Rye bread can be added to hasten fermentation. Today the sourness is often provided by sauerkraut juice, pickle brine, vinegar, citric acid crystals or a product called beet sour. The soup is served in small bowls or two-handled cups, along with little pastries. A vegetarian version is made with vegetable stock and sour beet juice, while sour cream is added to make a creamy one. Clear beet soup is sure to be on Christmas Eve menus, and will have *uszka* ("little ears") in it, small pasta squares that have been folded over a mushroom filling to form a triangle and pinched together at two ends to form a ring.

**batat** sweet potato; also called *słodki ziemniak*.

**baton czekoladowy** chocolate candy bar.

**bawarka** sweetened tea with milk.

**bazylia** basil.

**bażant** pheasant.

**bekas** snipe.

**bez** without.

**bez cukru** sugarless.

**bez lodu** without ice.

**beza** meringue.

**bezmięsny** meatless.

**biała fasola** navy bean.

**biała kapusta** green (white) cabbage.

**biała kawa** coffee with cream or milk.

**białe wino** white wine.

**białko** egg white.

**biały** white.

**biały pieprz** white pepper.

**biały ser** firm, dry, sliceable white farmer's cheese, the favorite cheese of Poles, which is used in sweet or savory dishes. Also called *twaróg*.

**biesiada** banquet or feast.

**biszkopt** sponge cake, biscuit, cracker or cookie.

**bita śmietana** whipped cream.

**bitki** pounded meat fillet.

**bobkowy** bay (leaf); also called *listek laurowe, listek bobkowy* and *liść laurowy*.

**bochenek** loaf.

**boczek** bacon.

**boćwina** Swiss chard; also means young beet greens.

**borowik** brown-capped, king bolete mushroom, which the Poles consider the tastiest of all. It is also called *prawdziwek* (true mushroom) and *grzyb prawdziwy*. See color insert, p. 5.

**borówka** lingonberry (mountain cranberry).

**borówka czernica** wild blueberry; also called *czernica* and *czarna jagoda*.

**bób** broad bean (fava bean).

**brokuły** broccoli; also called *kapusta szparagowa*.

**brukiew** rutabaga.

**brukselka** Brussels sprout.

**brusznica** a black berry known as whortleberry.

**bryndza** white, spreadable and somewhat granular sheep cheese made by mixing salt into old, soured *bunc,* a hard cheese made from sheep's milk; see *bunc,* this *Guide.*

**bryzol** pounded and fried tenderloin steak.

**brzoskwinia** peach.

**budyń** dessert pudding cooked in a mold in hot water.

**bulion wołowy** beef bouillon.

**bułeczka** small bread roll.

**bułka** bread roll; breakfast roll; white bread.

**bunc** hard, sweet, white sheep cheese with small holes, made by highland shepherds in the Gorce and Tatra Mountains in southern Poland. Curds formed by acidifying and heating sheep's milk are collected by straining the mixture through linen cloth, and then dried while still in the cloth sack. *Bunc* that will become the cheese called *oszczypek* is made from a mixture of cow's milk and sheep's milk. Before this *bunc* becomes completely dry, it is put in special spindle-shaped wooden molds that produce a decorative band at the middle of the spindle and at each conical end. *Oszczypek* (*oscypek* in the highlanders' dialect) is soaked in brine and slowly smoked for many days—even weeks—on shelves under the roofs of mountain cottages. This produces a brown skin on the cheese and rich, smoked flavor. Some *oszczypek* available today is not made the traditional way; only cow's milk is used and the brown color is produced by soaking the cheese in tea. Old *bunc* is used to make a softer, spreadable and somewhat granular cheese (*bryndza*) by stirring salt in it. See color insert, p. 4.

**burak** beet.
**butelka** bottle.
**butelka wina** bottle of wine.

**cebula** onion.
**cebulka** bulb (onion, shallot, etc.).
**chałka** braided, semi-sweet egg bread, a contribution to the cuisine from Polish Jews.
**chipsy** potato chips.
**chleb** bread.
**chleb razowy** whole-meal bread.
**chleb żytni** rye bread.
**chłop** peasant.
**chmiel** hops.
**chrupiący** crisp (adjective).
**chrupki** crisps (noun).
**chrzan** horseradish, usually used freshly grated.
**chuda szynka** lean ham.
**chude mieso** lean meat.
**ciastko** cake, cookie, pie or pastry.
**ciasto** dough.
**ciasto drożdżowe** yeast dough.
**ciasto francuskie** puff pastry.
**cielęcina** veal.
**ciemne piwo** dark beer.
**cierpki** tart, or sour; also called *kwaśny*.
**cietrzew** black grouse.
**comber** saddle or loin.
**comber sarni** saddle of venison.
**comber zajęczy** loin of hare.
**cukier** sugar.
**cukier buraczany** beet sugar.
**cukier puder** powdered sugar.
**cukier rafinowany** granulated sugar.
**cukier trzcinowy** cane sugar.
**cukierek** sweetmeat or candy.
**cukiernia** pastry shop.

cukinia zucchini squash.
cykoria chicory.
cynaderka kidney.
cynamon cinnamon.
cyranka garganey small, Old World duck.
cytryna lemon.
czarna jagoda wild blueberry; also called *borówka czernica* and *czernica*.
czarna kawa black coffee.
czarna porzeczka black currant.
czarnuszka black cumin.
czarny black.
czarny pieprz mielony ground black pepper.
cząber savory. This herb is widely used in the western Poznań region (Wielpolska).
czekolada chocolate.
czereśnia sweet cherry. The sour cherry is called *wiśnia*.
czernica wild blueberry; also called *borówka czernica* and *czarna jagoda*.
czerwona kapusta red cabbage.
czerwona porzeczka red currant.
czerwona sałata red lettuce.
czerwone wino red wine.
czerwony red.
czosnek garlic.
czysty clear; also *klarowny*.


daktyl date.
danie dish, course, serving of food.
danie barowe buffet dish.
danie główne main course.
danie gotowe dish prepared ahead.
danie jarskie vegetarian dish.
danie mięsne meat dish.
danie na zamówienie dish prepared while you wait.
danie rybne fish dish.
danie z drobiu poultry dish.
danie z dziczyzny game dish.
dania z jaj egg dish.

**deser** dessert.

**diablotki** cheese croutons.

**dodatki** side dishes or accompaniments.

**domowy** homemade.

**dorsz** cod.

**dropsy** fruit drops.

**drożdże** yeast.

**drożdże suche** dry yeast

**drożdże świeże** fresh yeast.

**drożdżowe paluszki** "yeast fingers;" filled or unfilled pastry often formed into a long roll from which individual servings are sliced.

**drożdżowka** brioche.

**drób** poultry.

**dróbki** giblets; also called *podróbki*.

**drugie śniadanie** "second breakfast" mid-morning snack, brunch or bag lunch (eaten at school or work).

**duszone** braised or stewed.

**dymka włoska** shallot; also called *szalotka*.

**dynia** pumpkin.

**dziczyzna** venison; can also refer to any wild game.

**dzik** wild boar.

**dzika gęs** wild goose.

**dzika kaczka** wild duck.

**dziki** wild.

**dżem** jam.

**endywia** endive.

**estragon** tarragon.

**farsz** stuffing; filling.

**fasola** bean.

**fasola jaś** lima bean; also called *jasiek* and sometimes *głupi jaś*.

**fasola sucha** dried bean.

**fasola szparagowa** wax bean.

**fasola złota** mung bean.

**faszerowany** stuffed.

**figa** fig.
**filet cielęcy** veal scallop.
**filiżanka** cup.
**flaki** tripe.
**flaki wołowe** beef tripe.
**flldra** flounder.
**frytki** French fries.

**galareta** jelly, gelatin or aspic.
**galeretka** small, molded gelatin desserts.
**gałka muszkatołowa** nutmeg; also called *muszkat*.
**gazowany** fizzy.
**gęś** goose.
**gicz** shank; also called *goleń*.
**głowa** head.
**głowizna** pig's head.
**głupi jaś** lima bean; also called *fasola jaś* and *jasiek*.
**głuszec** wood grouse.
**gofry** waffle.
**goleń** shank; also called *gicz*.
**golonka** pork shank, hock.
**gołąb** pigeon.
**gołębica** dove.
**gołębię** squab.
**gorące zakąski** small, hot hors d'oeuvres eaten with the fingers; also called *gorące przekąski*.
**gorąco** hot.
**gorczyca** white mustard.
**gorzki** bitter.
**gotowane** boiled.
**gotowane na parze** steamed.
**goździk** clove.
**grahamka** small, whole-wheat roll.
**granat** pomegranate.
**groch** pea. Refers primarily to dried yellow peas, which are used in soups, added to breads and served as a vegetable, mashed and formed into small, individual balls.

**groch cukrowy** sugar snap pea.

**groch ogrodowy** green pea; also called *zielony groszek*.

**groch włoski** chickpea.

**gruszka** pear.

**gryka** buckwheat; also called *hreczka* and *tatarka*. It is available whole, split or milled. The finest milled buckwheat is called *kasza krakowska*.

**grymasiki** type of tea cake.

**grysik** semolina; also called *kasza manna*.

**grzanka** toast.

**grzanki** crouton.

**grzyb** mushroom.

**grzyb prawdziwy** brown-capped, king bolete mushroom, which the Poles consider the tastiest of all. It is also called *borowik* and *prawdziwek*.

**gulasz** goulash; meat stew.

**herbaciarnia** tearoom.

**herbata** tea, usually prepared by mixing loose tea leaves with hot water, so one needs to let the tea leaves settle before drinking. Poles usually drink their tea without milk or cream, but often with lemon.

**herbata naturalna** tea without milk.

**herbata owocowa** fruit tea.

**herbata po angielsku** tea with milk.

**herbata z cytryną** tea with lemon.

**herbata ziołowa** herb tea.

**homar** lobster.

**hreczka** buckwheat; also called *gryka* and *tatarka*. It is available whole, split or milled. The finest milled buckwheat is called *kasza krakowska*.

**imbir** ginger.

**indyk** turkey.

**jabłecznik** apple cider; also called *wino z jabłek*.

**jabłko** apple.

**jadło** food, dish.

**jadłodajnia** basic, inexpensive eatery, diner or lunchroom.

**jadłospis** menu; also called *karta dań.*
**jagnię** lamb; also called *baranek* and *owieczka.*
**jagoda** berry.
**jajka przepiórcze** quail's egg.
**jajko** egg; also spelled *jajo.*
**jałowcówka** juniper-flavored vodka; also called *myśliwska.*
**jałowiec** juniper.
**jarmuż** kale.
**jarski** vegetarian.
**jarząbek** grouse.
**jarzębiak** rowanberry-flavored vodka.
**jarzębina** rowanberry (mountain ash).
**jarzyna** cooked vegetable. Also sometimes called *warzywo,* although this word means raw vegetable.
**jasiek** lima bean; also called *fasola jaś* and *głupi jaś.*
**jedzenie** food.
**jeleń** elk.
**jesiotr** sturgeon.
**jeżyna** blackberry.
**jęczmień** barley.


**kabanos** long, thin, dry-smoked pork sausage, eaten cold.
**kaczka** duck.
**kajzerka** small white roll.
**kakao** cocoa.
**kalafior** cauliflower.
**kalarepa** kohlrabi.
**kałamarnica** squid.
**kanapka** canapé.
**kandyzowany** candied.
**kania** umbrella mushroom.
**kantalupa** cantaloupe.
**kapar** caper.
**kapłon** capon.
**kapusta** cabbage.
**kapusta brukselka** Brussels sprout; also just called *brukselka.*
**kapusta kiszona** sauerkraut; also called *kapusta kwaszona.*

**kapusta szparagowa** broccoli; also called *brokuły*.

**kapusta włoska** savoy cabbage.

**karafka** carafe.

**karafka wina** carafe of wine.

**karaś** Old World panfish of the minnow family.

**karczma** an Old Polish word meaning an inn for travelers. Historically it was a place on the road where travelers could stop to change horses and have a bite to eat.

**karczoch** artichoke.

**kardamon** cardamom.

**kardy** chard.

**karkówa** meat from the lower neck.

**karmazyn** Norway haddock.

**karta dań** menu; also called *jadłospis*.

**kartofel** potato in eastern and central Poland. It is called *ziemniak* in the south and *pyrki* in the west. In the Tatra Mountain region the potato is called *grula,* which is more of a slang term comparable to the words spud and tater in the United States.

**kartoflane kluski** potato noodles.

**kartofle purée** mashed potatoes; also called *kartofle tłuczone*.

**kasza** groats; grits; porridge; gruel; also called *krupy*.

**kasza gryczana** buckwheat groats; also called *kasza hreczana*.

**kasza jaglana** millet groats; also called *proso*.

**kasza jęczmienna** barley groats.

**kasza krakowska** the finest milled buckwheat. Note that the general word for buckwheat is *gryka*.

**kasza kudurydziana** corn groats.

**kasza łamana** barley groats, coarsely cracked.

**kasza manna** semolina; also called *grysik*.

**kasza perłowa** pearl barley (milled and polished barley).

**kasza pszenna** wheat cereal.

**kaszanka** blood sausage. See *kiszka*.

**kasztan** chestnut.

**kawa** coffee. Poles often prepare *kawa turecka* (see below)and drink it black, after a meal or with dessert.

**kawa bezkofeinowa** decaffeinated coffee.

**kawa duża** large coffee.

**kawa espresso** steamed, filtered coffee served in demitasse.

**kawa mała** small coffee. In a café it is made on an espresso machine using twice the usual amount of water.

**kawa mrożona** iced coffee.

**kawa naturalna** strong black coffee.

**kawa po staropolsku** spiced coffee, Old Polish-style.

**kawa turecka** coffee prepared by mixing hot water with ground coffee. The grounds need to settle before drinking.

**kawa z mlekiem** coffee with milk.

**kawa zbożowa** ersatz coffee made from roasted barley, sugar beets and sometimes chicory.

**kawa ze śmietanką** coffee with cream.

**kawiarnia** coffeehouse; café. They are very popular, serving tea, cakes and ice cream in addition to coffee.

**kawior złocisty** golden salmon caviar.

**kawon** watermelon; also called *arbuz*.

**keks** fruitcake; tea cake.

**kelner** waiter.

**kelnerka** waitress.

**kieliszek** liqueur glass.

**kiełbasa** sausage. See recipe, p. 60.

**kiełbasa myśliwska** hunter's smoked pork sausage.

**kiełbasa na gorąco** hot sausage.

**kiełbasa szynkowa** ham sausage.

**kiełbasa wędzona** smoked sausage.

**kisiel** a traditional jelly-like dessert, often containing fruit, which is thickened with potato flour or cornstarch.

**kiszka** blood sausage made with pork and pork variety meats, buckwheat groats and pork blood. Also called *kaszanka, kiszka z krwią* and *krwawa kiszka*.

**kiszona kapusta** sour cabbage; sauerkraut.

**kiszony ogórek** brined (vinegar-free) dill pickle.

**klarowny** clear; also *czysty*.

**kleik** thin gruel made by boiling rice or some other grain in water for a long time; it usually is fed to those who are ill or on a bland diet.

**klops** minced meat; meat loaf.

**klopsiki** meatballs.

**kluski** noodles or dumplings.

**kluski francuskie** French dumplings served in clear soups.

**kluski kładzione** small egg batter dumplings served in non-clear soups, as an accompaniment to meat, or by itself with butter or gravy, etc.

**kluski krajane** egg noodles.

**kluski lane** noodles made by pouring a thin stream of egg batter into boiling water, often through a small-bore funnel.

**kluski pólfrancuskie** French egg dumplings served in creamy soups.

**kmin rzymski** cumin.

**kminek** caraway seeds.

**kminkówka** caraway vodka.

**knedle** filled or unfilled potato dumpling. The fillings can be sweet (fruit) or savory (meat, mushroom or cheese).

**kolacja** supper, the last meal of the day. It is usually a lighter meal than dinner (*obiad*).

**kolendra** coriander; also spelled *kolender*.

**kołacz** jelly roll filled with fruit and nuts, whose ends are brought together to form a ring.

**kołaczki** small rolls filled with fruit and nuts; also means cookies. Sometimes spelled *kołaczyki*.

**kołduny** small, round or semicircular pastas filled with either mutton and suet or mushrooms. They are boiled and served in soup. *Kołduny* is the Lithuanian name for *pierogi*. Not surprisingly, several Lithuanian dishes became part of the Polish culinary repertoire as a result of the Polish-Lithuanian union that began in the late 14th century and lasted 400 years.

**kompot** compote, a dessert of fruit cooked in sugar water. *Kompot* can also mean a beverage and a soup. The mixture becomes a beverage by increasing the proportion of water to sugar. It becomes a soup (*zupa z kompotu*) by thickening the sugar water with flour.

**konfitura** preserves.

**koniak** cognac.

**koper** dill; also called *koper ogrodowy*.

**koper włoski** fennel; also called Italian dill.

**koreczki** small, cold shish kebab appetizers; also called *korki*.

**korkociag** corkscrew.

**korniszon** cucumber (usually small) pickled in vinegar; gherkin.

**kostka lodu** ice cube.

**koszerny** kosher.

**kotlet** cutlet; chop.

**kotlet schabowy** breaded pork cutlet or chop, the number one menu choice for many Poles.

**kotlety mielone** minced meat; meat patties.

**koza** goat.

**kozieradka** fenugreek.

**kozioł** billy goat.

**koźlątko** kid.

**krab** crab.

**kremówki** cream puffs with sweet or savory fillings. Also called *ptysie*.

**krew** blood.

**krewetka** shrimp.

**krokiet** croquette; can also be a crêpe spread with a filling, rolled up like a jelly roll and fried.

**kromka** slice (of bread).

**królik** rabbit.

**krupnik** honey liqueur; also the name for barley and vegetable soup.

**krupy** groats; also called *kasza*.

**krwawa kiszka** blood sausage. See *kiszka*.

**krzyżowa** beef rump steak.

**kubek** mug.

**kuchnia** kitchen.

**kufel** beer mug.

**kukurydza** sweet corn.

**kulebiak** filled or unfilled pastry often formed into a long roll from which individual servings are sliced.

**kura** hen.

**kurczak** chicken; also spelled *kurczę*.

**kurka** golden chanterelle mushroom; also called *pieprznik jadalny*.

**kurkuma** turmeric.

**kuropatwa** partridge.

**kwasek cytrynowy** citric acid crystals.

**kwaśna żętyca** soured sheep's milk.

**kwaśne mleko** sour milk similar to buttermilk.

**kwaśnica** sauerkraut juice.

**kwaśny** tart or sour; also called *cierpki*.

**kwiat muszkatołowy** mace.


**lane** draft beer; also called *piwo beczkowe*.

**legumina** dessert; also a baked, non-molded pudding usually thickened with flour.

**leszcz** bream.
**likier** liquor.
**limona** lime.
**lin** tench (a fish).
**listek bobkowy** bayleaf; also called *listek laurowy*.
**liść** leaf; also called *listek*.
**lody** ice cream or fruit ices.
**lody mieszane** assorted ice cream or fruit ices.
**lód** ice.
**lubczyk** lovage.
**lukier** cake icing.

**łata** beef flank steak.
**łazanki** egg noodles cut in small squares.
**łopatka** shoulder.
**łopatka barania** lamb or mutton shoulder.
**łosoś** salmon.
**łoś** European elk.
**łój** suet.
**łuki** crescent roll; also called *rogal*.
**łupina** skin; rind.
**łyżeczka** teaspoon.
**łyżka** spoon.

**macierzanka** thyme; also called *tymianek*.
**majeranek** marjoram.
**majonez** mayonnaise.
**majonez chrzanowy** horseradish mayonnaise.
**mak** poppy seed.
**makaron** egg noodle.
**makrela** mackerel.
**malina** raspberry.
**mało wysmażone** food cooked underdone or rare.
**mamażyga** corn gruel.
**mandarynka** tangerine.
**marcepan** marzipan.

**marchew** carrot.

**margaryna** margarine.

**marmurek** marble cake.

**marynata** pickle; pickled vegetables.

**marynowany** marinated.

**masa** paste or filling; torte filling.

**masarnia** sausage shop; butcher shop selling pork.

**masło** butter.

**maszynka do kawy** coffee pot; espresso pot.

**maślak** butterball mushroom.

**maślanka** buttermilk.

**mazurek** flat, square or rectangular cake typically no more than an inch high. A small rim is made along the edges to accommodate toppings of countless variations. This cake is a traditional Easter specialty.

**mąka** flour.

**mąka kartoflana** potato flour.

**melasa** molasses or brown sugar.

**melon** honeydew melon.

**miałki** powdered; fine.

**miąższ** fruit pulp.

**mielone mięso** ground or minced meat; also called *siekanina*.

**mielonka** type of lunch meat similar to Spam.

**mieszanka warzywna** mixed vegetables.

**mięso** meat.

**mięso z ruszto** grilled meat.

**mięta** mint.

**migdał** almond.

**migdały prażone** roasted almonds.

**miodownik** gingerbread; also called *piernik*.

**miodówka** honey vodka.

**miód** honey.

**miód pitny** mead, an alcoholic beverage made by fermenting a mixture of honey and water.

**misa** large bowl.

**miseczka** very small bowl.

**miska** small bowl.

**mleczarnia** dairy; milk bar. Also see *bar mleczny*.

**mleko** milk.

**mocno wysmażone** food cooked "well done."

**morela** apricot.

**morszczuk** blue grenadier (fish).

**morwa** mulberry.

**mostek cielęcy** veal brisket.

**móżdżki** brains.

**mrożonka** frozen food.

**mule** mussels.

**mus** mousse.

**muszkat** nutmeg; also called *gałka muszkatołowa*.

**musztarda** mustard.

**myśliwska** hunter's sausage; a beef and pork sausage flavored with ground juniper berries and cured in juniper smoke. The sausage is typically eaten cold. *Myśliwska* is also the name for hunter's vodka, also called *jałowcówka,* which is flavored with juniper berries, the main flavoring agent of gin.

**na gorąco** served hot.

**na słodko** served as a sweet.

**na słono** served as a savory.

**na sypko** dry, not sticking together.

**na zimno** served cold.

**nadzienie** filling; stuffing.

**nadziewane** stuffed.

**naleśnik** crêpe that is folded or rolled around a filling and browned in butter or baked.

**nalewka** strong infusion of alcohol-steeped fruits, herbs or nuts.

**napitek** drink; also called *napój.*

**napiwek** tip; gratuity.

**napoje bezalkoholowe** non-alcoholic drinks.

**napoje wyskokowe** strong drink; tipple.

**napój** drink or beverage; also called *napitek.*

**napój jabłkowy** apple juice with mineral water.

**nasiona dyni** pumpkin seed; also called *pestki dyniowe.*

**nasiona kopru** dill seed.

**nasionko** seed.

**nektarynka** nectarine.

**nerkowiec** cashew; also called *orzech nanerczowy.*

**nerkówka cielęca** veal ribs.

**nie ma** (menu item) not available.

**niedogotowany** food that is "undercooked;" also called *niedosmażony*.

**niedojrzały** unripe.

**noga** leg, foot.

**nogi wieprzowe** pig's knuckles; pig's feet; trotters. Also called *nóżki wieprzowe*.

**nóż** knife.

**obiad** dinner, the main meal of the day; usually eaten between 1 and 5 PM.

**obiad firmowy** set menu; blue plate special.

**obiady domowe** home-cooked meals.

**obwarzanek** ring-shaped roll sprinkled with poppy seeds. It is a popular street food in Cracow. See color insert, p. 2.

**ocet** vinegar.

**ocet ziołowy** herb vinegar.

**ogon** tail.

**ogórek** cucumber.

**ogórek kiszony** cucumber pickled in brine. See recipe, p. 61.

**okoń** perch.

**olej** oil

**oliwa** olive oil.

**oliwka** olive.

**opłatek** Christmas wafer made of wheat flour, which is embossed with a religious motif on one side. Before eating the Christmas Eve meal (*wigilia*), the wafers are broken and shared among everyone present, with wishes for good health and God's blessings to all.

**orzech** nut.

**orzech kokosowy** coconut.

**orzech laskowy** hazelnut.

**orzech nanerczowy** cashew; also called *nerkowiec*.

**orzech pistacjowy** pistachio.

**orzech włoski** walnut.

**orzech ziemny** peanut.

**oskomian pospolity** starfruit.

**ostra papryka** cayenne pepper; also called *pieprz turecki*.

**ostrężnica** blackberry.

# FOODS & FLAVORS  GUIDE

**ostryga** oyster.

**oszczypek** molded, smoked sheep's milk cheese made in the Tatra Mountain region from *bunc* cheese before it is completely dry (see *bunc,* this *Guide*).

**ośmiornica** octopus.

**otręby** bran.

**owca** sheep.

**owieczka** lamb; also called *baranek* and *jagnię.*

**owies** oats.

**owoc** fruit.

**owoc kiwi** kiwi fruit.

**owsianka** oatmeal; kasha; porridge.

**ozorki** beef tongue.

**paluszek** stick cracker.

**paluszki słone** salty sticks.

**panierowany** in breadcrumbs; breaded.

**papryka** bell pepper.

**papryka słodka** paprika.

**parówka** hot dog; frankfurter.

**pasta** paste or spread.

**pasternak** parsnip.

**paszteciki** small pastries, pasties or turnovers, often with savory fillings, typically eaten with clear soups.

**pasztet** pâté, terrine or covered pie.

**pasztet domowy** homemade pâté.

**pasztetówka** liver sausage.

**patelnia** frying pan.

**patison** summer squash.

**pączki** filled doughnuts; some favorite fillings are plum/prune preserves and rose hips. They are eaten year round but never more so than on "Fat Thursday" before Ash Wednesday, when they assume great importance as a pre-Lenten carnival treat.

**pekińska kapusta** celery cabbage.

**perliczka** guinea fowl.

**pestka** fruit pit or stone.

**pestki** seeds.

**pestki dyni** pumpkin seeds; also called *nasiona dyni.*

**pęcak** hulled, whole-grained barley; also spelled *pęczak.*

**piec** stove.

**pieczarki** cultivated button mushrooms, the most common cooking mushrooms in the United States.

**pieczony** baked; roasted.

**pieczyste** roasted meat; roast.

**pieczywo** bread products; often considered a side dish on menus, and not included in the price of the meal.

**piekarnia** bakery.

**pieprz** pepper(corn).

**pieprz angielski** allspice, or English pepper; also called *ziele angielskie*.

**pieprz czarny** black pepper.

**pieprz turecki** cayenne pepper; also called *ostra papryka*.

**pieprznik jadalny** golden chanterelle mushroom; also called *kurka*.

**pieprzówka** pepper-flavored vodka, formerly a folk remedy for upset stomachs.

**piernik** gingerbread, or honey-spice cake, a Christmas specialty. Also called *miodownik*. The most renowned is from the city of Toruń (*pierniki torunski*). See color insert, p. 7.

**pierogi** thin circles of pasta dough topped on one side with sweet or savory fillings, then folded in half, sealed at the edges and boiled. Meat, sauerkraut, potatoes, cheese and fruit are typical fillings.

**pierożki** small *pierogi*.

**pierś** breast (poultry).

**pierś z kurczaka** chicken breast.

**pietruszka** parsley.

**pigwa** quince.

**piołunówka** absinthe-flavored liqueur.

**piskorz** long, slender fish with barbels.

**piwiarnia** beer bar.

**piwo** beer.

**piwo beczkowe** draft beer; also called *lane*.

**piwo butelkowe** bottled beer.

**piwo karmelowe** dark, alcohol-free beer.

**piwo słodowe** dark, alcohol-free malt beer.

**piwo w puszce** canned beer.

**placek** pie, tart or yeast-raised cake.

**placki** sweet breads; also the name for pancake.

**plasterek** slice (of cheese, ham, lemon, etc.). Note that a slice of bread is called *kromka*.

**płatny** for a fee.

**płuco** lung.

**po chłopsku** peasant style.

**po francusku** French style, often meaning in an egg, butter, flour and cream sauce.

**po góralsku** highlander style, often meaning that sheep's cheese made in the Tatra Mountain area is an ingredient.

**po królewsku** royal style; à la royale.

**po magnacku** aristocratic style.

**po polsku** Polish style, often meaning topped with sautéed, buttered bread-crumbs. When this term is used to describe poached fish, it implies that the fish is topped with chopped egg.

**po staropolsku** Old Polish style, often meaning spicy (cloves, ginger, cinnamon, pepper, saffron and caraway) with dried fruits, honey and poppy seeds. Another way to say Old Polish style is *staropolsku*.

**po wiejsku** country style.

**po włosku** Italian style, often meaning with tomato sauce and cheese.

**po żydowsku** Jewish style.

**pochrzyn** yam.

**podpiwek** alcohol-free dark beer.

**podróbki** giblets; also called *dróbki*.

**podudzia** leg (poultry).

**pokrzywa** nettle.

**polewka** cheese soup or gruel made of hot milk, water and fresh curds.

**polędwica** tenderloin.

**polędwica wołowa** beef tenderloin, often on menus as Chateaubriand.

**pomarańcza** orange.

**pomidor** tomato.

**pomidor winogronowy** cherry tomato.

**pomidor włoski** Italian plum tomato.

**poncz** punch; also the name for flavored torte liquor, a solution of spirits and flavorings added to moisten and flavor a torte.

**poncz owocowy** fruit punch.

**por** leek.

**porter** stout.

**porzeczka** currant.

**posiłek** meal.

**postny** Lenten.

**potrawa** dish or course.

**potrawa na gorąco** hot dish.

**potrawa na zimno** cold dish.

**potrawka** ragout; fricassee.

**potrawy jarskie** vegetable items on a menu; vegetarians should also look for the menu heading *bezmiesny* (meatless).

**potrawy mleczne i mlczne** dairy dishes.

**powidła** thick plum jam.

**poziomka** wild or alpine strawberry.

**pół butelki** half bottle.

**pół litra** half liter.

**półmisek** cold platter of something.

**półmisek firmowy** house platter of something.

**prawdziwek** brown-capped, king bolete mushroom, which the Poles consider the tastiest of all. It is also called *grzyb prawdziwy* and *borowik*. Italians call it *porcini*. It is sold fresh or dried. See color insert, p. 5.

**prażona kukurydza** popcorn.

**prażyć** grill; roast.

**pręga** beef shank.

**prosię** young pig.

**proso** millet groats; also called *kasza jaglana*.

**proszek do pieczenia** baking powder.

**przecier** purée.

**przekąski** cold finger food eaten at cocktail parties, as opposed to *przystawki* or *zakąski,* the hearty, cold appetizers eaten with silverware while seated.

**przekładaniec** layer cake.

**przepiórka** quail.

**przyprawa** seasoning, spice or condiment.

**przyprawa do zup w kostkach** bouillon cubes.

**przyprawa myśliwska** Polish hunter's seasoning. It is a mixture of spices and herbs used to help reduce the "gamey" taste of game. Typical components are juniper, marjoram, onion powder, garlic powder, caraway and allspice.

**przystawki** cold appetizers typically eaten with silverware while seated, as opposed to small, cold finger food (*przekąski*) eaten at cocktail parties. These heartier appetizers are also called *zakąski.*

**pstrąg** trout.

**pszenica** wheat (hulled).

**pszenżyto** Polish grain that is a cross between rye and wheat. It has more gluten than rye, which makes it an excellent bread flour.

**ptasie mleczko** type of candy made with milk.

**ptysie** cream puffs with sweet or savory fillings; also called *kremówki*.

**pularda** fattened chicken.

**pulpety** forcemeat balls.

**puszka piwa** can of beer.

**pyrki** potato in western Poland (Great Poland). It is called *kartofel* in eastern and central Poland and *ziemniak* in the south. In the Tatra Mountain region the potato is called *grula,* which is a colloquialism comparable to spud and tater in the United States.

**pyza** dumpling made of a mixture of grated, raw potatoes and cooked potatoes. Also called *kluski z tartych kartofli.* It can be plain or stuffed; round or with a dimpled center made with a finger.

**rabarbar** rhubarb; also called *rzewień*.

**rachunek** itemized, written bill (check) in a restaurant.

**rak** crayfish.

**ratafia** fruit liqueur.

**razowiec** brown bread; whole-meal bread.

**restauracja** restaurant.

**rodzynek** raisin; also called *rodzynka*.

**rogal** crescent roll; also called *łuki*.

**rogalik** small butterhorn or crescent roll.

**rogi** butterhorn roll.

**rosół** broth or clear soup.

**rozbratel** rib steak.

**rozmaryn** rosemary.

**rumianek** camomile.

**rumsztyk** rump steak.

**ruszt** grill (noun).

**ryba** fish.

**rydz** orange "milky cap" mushroom with a concave or depressed cap.

**rynek** market square.

**ryż** rice.

**ryż dziki** wild rice.

**rzepa** turnip.

**rzewień** rhubarb; also called *rabarbar*.

**rzeżucha** garden cress.
**rzodkiewka** radish.

**sadło** suet; lard. Also called *smalec*.
**salceson** head cheese.
**sałata** lettuce; current usage limits this word to mean lettuce, not a salad; also called *zielona sałata* (green lettuce).
**sałata głowiasta krucha** head lettuce.
**sałata rzymska** romaine lettuce.
**sałatka** cold salad of pre-cooked ingredients; an exception is a salad of fresh tomatoes (*sałatka z pomidorów*).
**sam spożywczy** supermarket; also can refer to small grocery stores. Another name for supermarket is *supersam*.
**sandacz** walleyed pike or perch-like fish.
**sardela** anchovy.
**sardynka** sardine.
**sarna** roe deer; the small, Old World deer.
**sarnina** venison.
**schab** pork loin.
**schabowa pieczeń** slice of roast pork loin.
**seler korzeniowy** celery root.
**seler naciowy** celery.
**ser** cheese.
**ser chudy** low-fat cheese.
**ser myśliwski** cheese smoked over juniper wood.
**ser śmietankowy** cream cheese.
**serce** heart.
**serdelek** knackwurst.
**serek wiejski** cottage cheese.
**sernik** cheesecake.
**serwatka** whey, by-product of cheese making used in soup and other dishes.
**serwetka** napkin.
**sezam** sesame.
**siekanina** minced meat or hash; another way to say this is *mielone mięso*.
**siekany** chopped, minced.
**sklep spożywczy** grocery store.
**skórka** rind; peel.

Foods & Flavors  Guide

**skórka pomarańczowa**  orange peel.

**skrzydełko**  wing.

**skrzydełko z kurczaka**  chicken wing.

**skwarek**  crackling; small piece of pork fat sautéed to a crisp.

**słodka żętyca**  sweet sheep's milk.

**słodki**  sweet.

**słodki ziemniak**  sweet potato; also called *batat*.

**słonina**  fat back; salt pork.

**słonka**  woodcock.

**Smacznego!**  Enjoy your meal!

**smalec**  lard; suet; also called *sadło*.

**smardz**  morel.

**smazone mięso**  fried meat.

**smażony**  fried.

**soczewica**  lentil.

**soda oczyszczona**  baking soda.

**sok**  juice.

**sok ananasowy**  pineapple juice.

**sok jabłkowy**  apple juice.

**sok malinowy**  raspberry juice.

**sok owocowy**  fruit juice.

**sok pomarańczowy**  orange juice.

**sok truskawkowy**  strawberry juice.

**sok wiśniowy**  sour cherry juice.

**sok z cytryny**  lemon juice.

**sok z czarnej porzeczki**  black currant juice.

**soki owocowe**  fruit syrup, used as a topping or sweetener.

**solanka**  brine; also means bread roll coated with coarse salt.

**solniczka**  salt shaker.

**solony**  salted or salt-cured.

**soplica**  golden colored, flavored, dry vodka.

**sos cebulowy**  onion sauce.

**sos chrzanowy gorący**  hot horseradish sauce.

**sos chrzanowy zimny**  cold horseradish sauce.

**sos grzybowy**  mushroom sauce.

**sos grzybowy ze śmietaną**  sour cream and mushroom sauce.

**sos jałowcowy**  juniper berry sauce.

**sos kaparowy biały**  white caper sauce.

**sos koperkowy** dill sauce.

**sos mięsny** gravy or meat sauce.

**sos ogórkowy** dill pickle sauce.

**sos pieczarkowy** fresh mushroom sauce.

**sos polski szary** Polish gray sauce. This sweet-sour sauce, which is actually brown, contains gingerbread, almonds, raisins, wine and caramelized sugar, and is typically served with fresh or smoked tongue or with carp; also called *szary sos staropolski* or *szary sos polski.*

**sos pomidorowy** tomato sauce.

**sos szczawiowy** sorrel sauce.

**sos szczypiorkowy** chive sauce.

**sos śmietanowy** sour cream sauce.

**sos tatarski** tartar sauce.

**sól** salt.

**sól gruba** coarse Kosher salt.

**sól kuchenna** table salt.

**specjalność kuchni** house speciality; also called *specjalność zakładu.*

**spirytus** high-proof alcohol.

**spodek** saucer.

**staropulsku** see *po staropolsku.*

**statki** kitchen utensils.

**stolik** table.

**strucla** strudel.

**suchar** cracker.

**suchy** dry.

**sum** large, freshwater catfish.

**sumik** bullhead.

**supersam** supermarket; also can refer to small grocery stores. Another name for supermarket is *sam spożywczy.*

**surowy** raw.

**surówka** dinner salad made with raw or pickled vegetables and fresh salad greens.

**suszone** dried.

**suszone grzyby** dried mushrooms.

**syrop** syrup.

**szafran** saffron.

**szalotka** shallot; also called *dymka wołske.*

**szałwia** sage.

**szampan** champagne.

**szary** gray.

**szczaw** sorrel.

**szczupak** northern pike.

**szczypiorek** chive.

**szklanka** drinking glass.

**sznycel** veal cutlet.

**szparag** asparagus.

**szpik** marrow.

**szpinak** spinach.

**szprot** sprat (a fish).

**sztuczne środki słodzące** artificial sweeteners.

**szyja** neck.

**szynka** ham.

**szynka gotowana** boiled ham.

**szynka gotowana, na zimno** cold boiled ham.


**śledź** herring.

**ślimak** snail.

**śliwka** plum.

**śliwka suszona** prune.

**śliwka węgierka** Hungarian plum; also called simply *węgierka*. For reasons that have faded from memory, the common plum grown in Poland is called the Hungarian plum.

**śliwowica** liquor made from plums.

**śmietana** sour cream; clotted cream.

**śmietanka** sweet cream.

**śmietanka chuda** half and half.

**śniadanie** breakfast.

**średnio wysmażone** food cooked "medium well."

**świeży** fresh, raw.

**święcone** traditional Easter meal of foods blessed the day before.


**talerz** plate.

**talerz głęboki** soup plate.

**talerz płytki** dinner plate.

**tarta bułka** breadcrumbs.

**tarty** grated.

**tatarka** buckwheat; also called *gryka* and *hreczka*. It is available whole, split or milled. The finest milled buckwheat is called *kasza krakowska*.

**topinambur** Jerusalem artichoke.

**tort** torte or multi-layered cake.

**trunek** alcoholic drink.

**truskawka** strawberry.

**trybula** chervil.

**trzustka** sweetbread (pancreas).

**tuńczyk** tuna fish.

**twarożek** cottage cheese; soft, white, crumbly curd cheese.

**twaróg** firm, dry, sliceable farmer's cheese, the favorite cheese of Poles, which is used in countless sweet and savory dishes. Also called *biały ser* (white cheese).

**tymianek** thyme; also called *macierzanka*.

**tzatziki** sauce made with cucumber, garlic and yogurt.

**udko** thigh (poultry).

**udko z kurczaka** chicken thigh.

**udziec** haunch or leg.

**udziec sarni** deer haunch.

**uszka** "little ears," small pasta squares that have been folded over a mushroom or meat filling to form a triangle, which is then pinched together at two ends to form a ring. They are served in beet soup (*barszcz*). *Uszka* with mushrooms are served in clear *barszcz* on Christmas Eve.

**w galarecie** in aspic.

**wanilia** vanilla.

**warzywo** raw vegetable; sometimes also called *jarzyna,* although strictly this word means cooked vegetable.

**watróbka** liver.

**wegetarianin** vegetarian.

**wędlina** smoked pork meat product.

**wędliniarnia** smoked pork butcher shop.

**wędzone mięso** smoked meat.

**wędzonka** smoked bacon.

**wędzony** smoked.

**węgierka**  Hungarian plum; also known as *śliwka węgierka*. For reasons that have faded from memory, the common plum grown in Poland is called the Hungarian plum.

**węgorz**  eel.

**widelec**  fork.

**wieprzowina**  pork.

**wigilia**  traditional Christmas Eve meal.

**wino**  wine.

**wino deserowe**  dessert wine.

**wino domowej roboty**  homemade wine.

**wino grzane**  mulled wine.

**wino słodkie**  sweet wine

**wino wytrawne**  dry wine.

**wino z jabłek**  apple cider; also called *jabłecznik*.

**winogrona**  grape.

**wiśnia**  sour cherry; the sweet cherry is called *czereśnia*.

**wiśniak**  cherry liqueur.

**wiśniówka**  sweet, cherry-flavored vodka.

**włoszczyzna**  soup stock vegetables.

**woda**  water.

**woda mineralna**  mineral water.

**woda sodowa**  soda water.

**wołowina**  beef.

**wódka**  vodka.

**wódka czysta**  clear vodka.

**wyborowa**  dry, clear vodka made from rye grain spirits.

**wystałe piwo**  lager.

**wytrawne wino**  dry wine.

**wywar**  stock (soup).

**wywar z mięsa**  meat stock.

**wywar z włoszczyzny**  vegetable stock.

**z cukrem**  with sugar.

**z cytryną**  with lemon.

**z grilla**  barbecued.

**z lodem**  with ice.

**z mlekiem** with milk.

**z rusztu** grilled.

**z wody** boiled in water.

**zając** hare.

**zakąski** hearty cold appetizers eaten with silverware while seated, as opposed to small, also cold, finger food (*przekąski*) eaten at cocktail parties. Also called *przystawki*.

**zakwas** sour liquid made with rye, oatmeal or bread, used as a souring agent for dishes requiring tartness. It is used to prepare the classic soup *żurek*.

**zapiekana** casserole.

**zaprawa z octu i przypraw** vinegar and herb marinade.

**zaprawa z samego wina** wine marinade.

**ze śmietanką** with cream.

**zestaw firmowy** a restaurant's set menu of special dishes.

**zestaw obiadowy** full-course dinner special.

**zestaw ziół** mixed herbs.

**ziele angielskie** allspice, or English pepper; also called *pieprz angielski*.

**zielona cebula** scallion.

**zielona fasola** green bean or pole bean; also called *zielona fasola szparagowa*.

**zielona sałata** lettuce; also simply called *sałata*.

**zielony** green.

**zielony groszek** fresh green pea; also called *groch ogrodowy*.

**ziemniak** potato in southern Poland. It is called *kartofel* in eastern and central Poland, and *pyrki* in the west. In the Tatra Mountain region the potato is called *grula,* which is a colloquialism comparable to the words spud and tater in the United States.

**ziemniak młody** new potato.

**zimno** cold.

**zimny sos pomidorowy** cold tomato sauce.

**zioło** herb.

**zraz** pounded fillet of meat, which may be rolled around a filling before it is cooked.

**zsiadłe mleko** sour milk; a popular and refreshing drink by itself, or the basis for milk shakes. It is also enjoyed with potatoes or groats.

**zupa** soup.

**zupa goraca** hot soups.

**zupa zimna** cold soup.

**zwierzyna** game.

**żaba** frog.

**żeberka** ribs.

**żelatyna** jelly.

**żerdka** small perch.

**żołądka** gizzard.

**żółta fasola szparagowa** wax bean; also simply called *fasola szparagowa*.

**żółtko** yolk.

**żółty** yellow.

**żółty ser** yellow cheese.

**żubr** bison.

**żubrówka** vodka flavored with a blade of bison grass. It is traditionally drunk with apple juice.

**żur** sour rye juice, the basis for sour rye soup (*żurek*). See *Menu Guide*.

**żurawina** cranberry.

**żytnia** dry, clear rye vodka.

**żytniówka** corn or rye vodka; gin.

**żyto** rye.

# Bibliography

Ascherson, Neal. *The Struggles for Poland.* New York: Random House, 1987.

Benet, Sula. *Song, Dance, and Customs of Peasant Poland.* New York: Roy Publishers, 1951.

Bjärvall, Anders and Staffan Ullström. *The Mammals of Britain and Europe.* London: Croom Helm, 1986.

Bogucki, Peter and Ryszard Grygiel. The First Farmers of Central Europe: A Survey Article. In *Journal of Field Archaeology,* Vol. 20, pp. 399–426. Boston: Boston University, 1993.

Bromke, Adam. *The Meaning and Uses of Polish History.* Boulder, Colorado: East European Monographs, 1987.

Cantrell, Rose. *Polish Cooking.* New York: Weathervane Books, 1978.

Chmielewski, Piotr. Mountain Commons in the Tatras. In *International Association for the Study of Common Property,* Papers of the Fifth Annual Conference, no. 9, 1995.

Cierlinska, Hanna, production editor. *Panorama of Polish History.* Warsaw: Interpress Publishers, 1982.

Coleman, Marion Moore. *Zosia and Thaddeus or An Ancient Feud Ended.* Cheshire, Connecticut: Cherry Hill Books, 1974.

Corley, Sherrill, editor. *Polish Cookbook.* Chicago: Culinary Arts Institute, 1976.

Courtenay, Booth and Harold H. Burdsall, Jr. *A Field Guide to Mushrooms and Their Relatives.* New York: Van Nostrand Reinhold Company, 1982.

Davies, Norman. *God's Playground: A History of Poland.* Vol. I, The Origins to 1795. New York: Columbia University Press, 1984.

Davies, Norman. *God's Playground: A History of Poland.* Vol. II, 1795 to the Present. New York: Columbia University Press, 1982.

Dembińska, Maria. *Food and Drink in Medieval Poland: Rediscovering a Cuisine of the Past.* Translated by Magdalena Thomas; revised and adapted by William Woys Weaver. Philadelphia, Pennsylvania: University of Pennsylvania Press, 1999.

Duplaix, Nicole and Noel Simon. *World Guide to Mammals.* New York: Crown Publishers, Inc., 1976.

Dvornik, Francis. *Byzantine Missions among the Slavs: SS.Constantine and Methodius.* New Brunswick, New Jersey: Rutgers University Press, 1970.

Dvornik, Francis. *The Slavs: Their Early History and Civilization.* Boston: American Academy of Arts and Sciences, 1956.

Fedorowicz, J.K., Maria Bogucka and Henryk Samsonowicz, editors. *A Republic of Nobles: Studies in Polish History to 1864.* Cambridge, England: Cambridge University Press, 1982.

Giełżyński, Wojciech. *Poland.* Warsaw, Poland: Arkady, 1975.

Górka, Olgierd. *Outline of Polish History: Past and Present.* London: Alliance Press Limited, 1945.

Grey-Wilson, Christopher. *Poppies: The Poppy Family in the Wild and in Cultivation.* Portland, Oregon: Timber Press, 1993.

Grudzinski, Tadeusz. *Boleslaus the Bold, Called Also the Bountiful, and Bishop Stanislaus: The Story of a Conflict.* Translated by Lech Petrowicz. Warsaw, Poland: Interpress Publishers, 1985.

Halecki, O. *A History of Poland.* London: Routledge & Kegan Paul, Ltd, 1978.

Heberle, Marianna Olszewska. *Polish Cooking,* revised edition. Tucson, Arizona: HPBooks, Inc., 1991.

Heine, Marc E. *Poland.* New York: Hippocrene Books, 1981.

Jażdżewski, Konrad. *Poland: Ancient Peoples and Places.* London: Thames and Hudson, 1965.

Jordan, Alexander. *Insiders' Guide to Poland.* New York: Hippocrene Books, 1989.

Kalaida, Lydia B. *Slavic Cookery.* Madison, Wisconsin: University of Wisconsin Department of Slavic Languages, 1978.

Knab, Sophie Hodorowicz. *Polish Customs, Traditions and Folklore.* New York: Hippocrene Books, 1993.

Knab, Sophie Hodorowicz. *Polish Herbs, Flowers & Folk Medicine.* New York: Hippocrene Books, 1995.

Korzycka-Iwanow, Malgorzata. Ownership Transformations in Polish Agriculture. In *International Association for the Study of Common Property*, Papers of the Fifth Annual Conference, no. 29, 1995.

Kostrowicki, Jerzy and Roman Szczęsny. *Polish Agriculture: Characteristics, Types and Regions.* Budapest: Akadémiai Kiadó, 1972.

Kuczyńska, Teresa. *Souvenir of Poland.* Translated by Louise Wędrychowska. Warsaw, Poland: Interpress Publishers, 1978.

Kwasowska, Bernadeta and Alicja Zagórska, editors. *Kuchnia Polska Regionalna.* Łomża, Poland: Oficyna Wydawnicza, 1989.

Lemnis, Maria and Henryk Vitry. *Old Polish Traditions in the Kitchen and at the Table.* New York: Hippocrene Books, 1996.

Lipniacka, Ewa. *Xenophobe's Guide to the Poles.* West Sussex, England: Ravette Publishing, Ltd., 1994.

Lorentz, Fr., Adam Fischer and Tadeusz Lehr-Spławiński. *The Cassubian Civilization.* London: Faber and Faber Ltd, 1935.

Łebkowska, Danuta and Marek. *Grzyby. Encyklopedia Sztuki Kulinarnej, 51.* Warsaw, Poland: Wydawnictwo Tenten, 1998.

Librowska, Maria, editor. *Kuchnia Polska.* Warsaw, Poland: Państwowe Wydawnictwo Ekonomiczne, 1974.

McKenny, Margaret. *The Savory Wild Mushroom.* Revised and enlarged by Daniel E. Stuntz. Seattle, Washington: University of Washington Press, 1971.

Michener, James A. *Pilgrimage: A Memoir of Poland & Rome.* Emmaus, Pennsylvania: Rodale Press, 1990.

Michener, James A. *Poland.* New York: Ballantine Books, 1983.

Mickiewicz, Adam. *Pan Tadeusz or The Last Foray in Lithuania.* Translated by Kenneth Mackenzie. London: The Polish Cultural Foundation, 1986.

Miller, J. Innes. *The Spice Trade of the Roman Empire: 29 B.C. to A.D. 641.* London: Oxford University Press, 1969.

Nowak, Ronald M. and John L. Paradiso. *Walker's Mammals of the World,* Volume II, 2nd edition. Baltimore, MD: The Johns Hopkins University Press, 1983.

Nowakowski, Jacek and Marlene Perrin, editors. *Polish Touches: Recipes and Traditions.* Iowa City, Iowa: Penfield Press, 1996.

Ochorowicz-Monatowa, Marja. *Polish Cookery.* Translated by Jean Karsavina. New York: Crown Publishers, Inc., 1958.

Pinińska, Mary. *Little Polish Cookbook.* San Francisco, California: Chronicle Books, 1992.

Pogonowski, Iwo Cypria. *Poland: A Historical Atlas.* New York: Hippocrene Books, 1987.

Polanie Club. *Treasured Polish Recipes for Americans.* Minneapolis, Minnesota: Polanie Publishing Company, 1948.

Pokropek, Marian. *Guide to Folkart and Folklore in Poland.* Translated by Magdalenea Mierowska Paszkiewicz. Warsaw, Poland: Arkady, 1980.

Puzdrowska, Krystyna, editor. *Kuchnia Pomorska.* Gdańsk, Poland: Ośrodek Doradztwa Rolniczego, 1998.

Reddaway, W. F., J. H. Penson, O. Halecki and R. Dyboski, editors. *The Cambridge History of Poland: From Augustus II to Piłsudski (1697–1935).* London: Cambridge University Press, 1951.

Reddaway, W. F, J. H. Penson, O. Halecki and R. Dyboski, editors. *The Cambridge History of Poland: From the Origins to Sobieski.* London: Cambridge University Press, 1950.

Reymont, Ladislas. *The Peasants: A Tale of Our Times.* In four volumes: Autumn, Winter, Spring and Summer. Translated by Michael H. Dziewicki. New York: Alfred A. Knopf, 1925.

Rubinstein, Nela. *Nela's Cookbook.* New York: Alfred A. Knopf, 1983.

Rysia. *Old Warsaw Cook Book: Hundreds of Polish Specialties with Many Additions from Cuisines the World Over.* New York: Roy Publishers, 1958.

Schenker, Alexander M. *The Dawn of Slavic: An Introduction to Slavic Philology.* New Haven, Connecticut: Yale University Press, 1995.

Stevens, Christopher and Jane Kennan, editors. *Reform in Eastern Europe and the Developing Country Dimension.* London: Overseas Development Institute, 1992.

Strybel, Robert and Maria. *Polish Heritage Cookery.* New York: Hippocrene Books, 1997.

Styczyński, Jan. *Vistula: The Story of a River.* Warsaw, Poland: Interpress Publishers, 1973.

Super, Paul. *Events and Personalities in Polish History.* London: The Baltic Institute, 1936.

Szafer, Władysław. *Concise History of Botany in Cracow Against the Background of Six Centuries of the Jagiellonian University.* Translated by Witold Kulerski and Halina Markiewicz. Warsaw, Poland: The Scientific Publications Foreign Cooperation Center of the Central Institute for Scientific, Technical and Economic Information, 1969.

Sznajder, Michal and Benjamin Senauer. *The Changing Polish Food Consumer.* Working paper 98-02. University of Minnesota: Retail Food Industry Center, 1998.

Terofal, Fritz and Claus Militz. *Ryby Słodkowodne.* Warsaw, Poland: Świat Książki, 1997.

Walczak, Małgorzata and Michael Jacobs. *Polish Cooking.* Warsaw, Poland: Exlibris, 1998.

Ward, Philip. *Polish Cities: Travels in Cracow and the South, Gdansk, Malbork, and Warsaw.* Gretna, Louisiana: Pelican Publishing Company, Inc., 1989.

West, Karen. *The Best of Polish Cooking.* New York: Hippocrene Books, Inc., 1991.

Wojciechowska, Izabella. *Kuchnia Śląska.* Katowice, Poland: Videograf II, 1996.

Woronowicz, Leon. *English-Polish and Polish-English Agricultural Dictionary.* London: The Polish Farmers' Association in Great Britian, 1959.

Zamoyski, Adam. *The Polish Way: A Thousand-year History of the Poles and Their Culture.* New York: Hippocrene Books, 1994.

Żerańska, Alina. *The Art of Polish Cooking.* New York: Doubleday & Company, Inc., 1968.

# Index

# ORDER FORM

Use this form to order additional copies of **Eat Smart in Poland** or to order any of the other guidebooks in our **Eat Smart** series.

**Please send me:**

_____copies of   **Eat Smart in Poland:** How to Decipher the Menu, Know the Market Foods and Embark on a Tasting Adventure

_____copies of   **Eat Smart in Mexico:** How to Decipher the Menu, Know the Market Foods and Embark on a Tasting Adventure

_____copies of   **Eat Smart in Indonesia:** How to Decipher the Menu, Know the Market Foods and Embark on a Tasting Adventure

_____copies of   **Eat Smart in Turkey:** How to Decipher the Menu, Know the Market Foods and Embark on a Tasting Adventure

_____copies of   **Eat Smart in Brazil:** How to Decipher the Menu, Know the Market Foods and Embark on a Tasting Adventure

Each book is $12.95. Add $2.00 postage for one book, $1.00 for each additional book. Wisconsin residents add 5% sales tax. For international orders, please inquire about postal charges.

Check enclosed for   $ _____

Please charge my: **VISA**_____     **MASTERCARD**_____

Card # _____ Exp. Date: _____

_____

Signature

Name: _____

Address: _____

City: _____ State: _____ Zip: _____

Telephone: _____

Email: _____     Ginkgo Press™ Inc.
P. O. Box 5346
Madison, Wisconsin 53705
Tel: 608-233-5488  Fax: 608-233-0053
http://www.ginkgopress.com
**Mail this form to:**     ginkgo@ginkgopress.com

*design*   Ekeby
*cover design*   Susan P. Chwae
*color separations*   Widen Enterprises
*printing*   Thomson-Shore, Inc.

*typefaces*   Garamond Simoncini and Helvetica Black
*paper*   60 lb Joy White